DARK STATE

Democracy's Sunset

MIGUEL SOTO

ISBN: 979-8-9874830-4-6

Printed in the United States of America

Inspire the current social, Economic,
and Political situation in the US (2025-2026).

CHAPTER 1

AN AUTOCRATIC WORLD

Peaceful Life.

The living room exudes a cozy charm, featuring a generous sectional couch that invites relaxation, flanked by two plush recliners at either end, both facing a sleek, wall-mounted 75-inch TV that flickers softly in the dim light. The television, aglow with images, casts a warm, inviting glow that enhances the room's intimate atmosphere. At the center, a rustic wooden coffee table sits, surrounded by a pair of elegant swivel chairs, creating an inviting nook perfect for conversation or a movie night. The walls are adorned with tasteful decor, and the air hums with a sense of comfort, reminiscent of a quaint theater setting. A classic pendulum clock, its brass accents gleaming softly, ticks steadily in the background, its hands frozen at 7:00 p.m., adding a timeless quality to the scene.

Adam Reyes, a spirited systems engineer in his early 30s, reclines comfortably on the plush couch alongside his wife, Elena Reyes, a passionate journalist in her 30s. The living room vibrates with excitement as they gather with close friends and neighbors, their laughter and camaraderie filling the air. On the screen before them, a thrilling world-class soccer match unfolds, capturing their rapt attention. As the players skillfully navigate the field, Adam and Elena share playful banter and cheers, their enthusiasm a testament to their love for sports. Surrounded by snacks and drinks, the family finds joy not just in the game but also in their shared moments of watching shows and movies, creating lasting memories together.

The walls are lined with sturdy bookshelves, brimming with books in various shapes and sizes, transforming the space into a charming mini library that beckons studious minds. The warm glow of soft lighting creates a tranquil atmosphere, perfect for quiet contemplation and focus.

As the final whistle of the soccer game blows, laughter and chatter fade away, and friends and neighbors begin to drift out, their spirits high. Marta and Elena, with a sense of camaraderie and responsibility, set to work collecting empty bottles, discarded cups, and bits of trash. Their diligent efforts not only restore order but also leave the area neat and inviting, a testament to their care for the space they all shared.

Adam and Elena, married for just eight years, have cultivated a vibrant and fulfilling life together. At the bustling city community center, Adam showcases his expertise by teaching invaluable home maintenance and handyman skills. His engaging workshops empower individuals with the knowledge to tackle DIY projects with confidence. Meanwhile, Elena lights up the room as she shares her passion for languages and dance, guiding her students through the rhythm of words and movement.

Both Adam and Elena are ardent supporters of the arts, believing in their power to enrich lives. They often bring their lively karaoke equipment to the community center hall, transforming ordinary gatherings into exuberant celebrations. Their performances delight a diverse audience, including adults, disabled veterans, and senior citizens, creating a warm, inclusive atmosphere that fosters joy and connection among all who attend. Through their efforts, Adam and Elena not only teach skills but also build a strong sense of community and togetherness.

Adam is a dedicated professional at a consulting firm, specializing in developing efficient industrial processes and meticulous construction planning. His family life is characterized by a well-organized, steady routine, reflecting their commitment to stability and to nurturing a supportive environment. Though they tend to steer clear of the tumultuous waters of politics, they are deeply invested in their community, actively participating in local events and lending a helping hand to friends and neighbors in their endeavors.

A year and a half after their joyful wedding, Elena decided to take a leave of absence from her dynamic role at Popular TV Network, affectionately known as P-TV-N. This sabbatical was primarily to devote herself to the rewarding journey of motherhood as they welcomed their first baby. However, her time at home extended further with the exciting news of a second child on the way. Fast forward eight years, and their household is filled with the laughter of two delightful children: five-year-old Timothy, or Tim as he likes to be called, and four-year-old Sofia, who is eagerly attending pre-K. Their home resonates with the vibrant energy and joyful chaos of raising young kids.

Adam and Elena nestled together on their plush sectional couch, the soft fabric enveloping them like a warm embrace, as they settled in to watch the evening news. The flickering light from the television danced across their faces, illuminating the tranquility of the moment. Elena let out a gentle sigh, her breath a mix of contentment and reflection. Outside, the world bustled on, but within the cozy confines of their living room, a beautiful and serene atmosphere enveloped them—a testament to their love for each other and their deep appreciation for life's simple joys. As they held each other close, their hearts intertwined, they exchanged tender hugs and sweet kisses, radiating happiness in their own little oasis.

ELENA: (sighs) We have accomplished a lot in our eight years of marriage.

ADAM: Yes, but we've worked hard.

Adam and Elena cuddle. Elena looks around; everything is in its proper place.

ELENA: (sighs) Oh, the time goes by fast. It seems like we met yesterday at the beach party in Santa Monica, remember?

ADAM: Yes, that was (pause) when you asked me if I would marry you.

ELENA: That's not true. You proposed to me three times, and on the third time, I finally said yes. I gave you a chance. Crazy!

Adam and Elena are two diligent individuals who consistently embody a 'get-it-done' attitude, propelling them through daily challenges. Their commitment to hard work extends beyond their personal ambitions; they are generous with their knowledge and resources, eager to support those around them. Adam is the epitome of helpfulness, always ready to lend a hand or offer assistance when someone needs help. In contrast, Elena radiates warmth and compassion, her caring nature evident in every interaction. Together, they instill these invaluable principles in their children, nurturing a sense of responsibility and generosity within their family.

As time passes, circumstances and opportunities shift, and their lives begin to evolve in new and unexpected ways. Elena, reflecting on her past experiences and passions, contemplates a return to journalism, reigniting a dormant ambition.

ELENA: (sighs) The kids are growing up, getting ready to go to grade school!

ADAM: Ok, ok. What's the point?

ELENA: Well, let me explain. Elena sits up. The point is that I'm considering going back to journalism. Got it?

ADAM: My goodness, I could have said yes, do it, the first time you said it. Why did you hold it back?

Elena, surprised, looks at him, pauses, then says.

Elena: Okay! I'll start looking right away… tomorrow.

ADAM: Yes, dear, if that makes you happy!

Though not wealthy, they enjoy a life filled with comfort and contentment. In this cozy moment, Elena snuggles into the warmth of Adam's embrace as they sink into the soft cushions of the couch. A playful spark lights up Adam's eyes as he gently tickles her ribs, prompting fits of laughter that echo in the room. Their giggles intertwine, creating a melody of joy that fills the air, making every second feel magical. Yet, like the flickering flame of a candle, happiness is fleeting; it arrives in bursts, illuminating their lives, only to fade away moments later.

ON THE TV.

Breaking news catches their attention.

TV ANCHOR: Breaking news! Today, July 1st, 2025, at 2:00 P.M., people march in the streets of LA, protesting the government's illegal detentions and deportations. Three lawyers hurry out of a car and walk up the stairs to the Courthouse entrance. News reporters rush to interview them.

TV ANCHOR: Sir, can you tell us what brings you to this court today?

The reporter poses a question to clarify the government's socio-political situation. The lawyer continues walking but pauses to respond.

LAWYER: Today, we'll introduce a motion to stay the deportation of Kilmar Abrego-Garcia.

TV ANCHOR: Is this Kilmar's case critical?

LAWYER: The situation at hand raises significant concerns regarding the potential abuse of power by the government, which could have profound implications for liberty and democracy. The United States has a robust political system that has endured for 250 years, built upon a foundation of valued democratic principles and the rule of law. Current government actions appear to threaten these established norms and raise questions about the integrity of our justice system. Understanding this case is crucial, as it reflects broader issues about the preservation of democratic values and legal accountability.

TV ANCHOR: There it is. You heard it. Kilmar Abrego Garcia was arrested and deported to a foreign country without due legal process. Some other citizens may face the same treatment from the government.

IN THE LIVING ROOM.

ROBERT REYES, Salvadoran, in his mid-70s, a retired traveling sales manager for the Central American region, and MARTA REYES, a LA County Library System retiree, in her late 60s, come from the dining room to join Adam and Elena.

Robert is acutely aware of the patterns and tactics employed by dictators. Having firsthand experience living under oppressive regimes in Central America, he knows all too well the fear and uncertainty that accompany such rule. The memories of state-sanctioned violence, censorship, and the erosion of civil liberties weigh heavily on him. Now, as he observes a so-called "Wannabe-dictator" attempting to seize control in the United States, dismantling the intricate structure of government and undermining the very foundations of democracy, his concern deepens. The erosion of democratic norms, the rise of autocratic rhetoric, and the deliberate attacks on institutions that safeguard freedom disturb him profoundly. Robert is not just upset; he is alarmed for the future of democracy in his country and is motivated to speak out against the impending threat.

ROBERT: I've seen this movie before: a wannabe dictator, taking over the country, threatening this democracy.

Robert is absolutely right; if the president continues to evade accountability for his abuse of power and successfully instills fear among the populace, the very essence of democracy could vanish from this world.

Marta has stood steadfastly by her husband Robert's side throughout numerous trials and tribulations in various countries. Now, they find themselves navigating a new chapter in the United States. After years of perseverance and resilience, Robert and Marta have proudly become naturalized citizens, embracing the opportunities and responsibilities that come with their new status.

> MARTA: The situation gets worse every day-unemployment, cost of living. The saying "the richer gets richer, and the poor get poorer" proves true.

ON THE TV.

> TV ANCHOR: The president ignores the court orders. He has said he is the law; besides, he considers himself to have absolute immunity for all he does as president. Let's watch what a previous report said.

Flashback to the day before.

The sun shines brightly over Los Angeles at 9:30 A.M., casting a warm golden hue across the bustling city. A news helicopter circles overhead, its rotors slicing through the crisp morning air as it captures the scene below. The streets around the courthouse are alive with tens of thousands of furious protesters, their voices rising in a powerful chorus of anger and determination. Banners wave vigorously, painted with bold slogans, while the crowd pulses like a living organism, full of energy and urgency. With no traffic control in sight, chaos reigns on the nearby streets as cars inch their way around the mass of bodies. Police officers stand vigilantly at the building entrances, their uniforms a stark contrast to the vibrant display of dissent surrounding them, ready to maintain order amidst the swelling tide of unrest.

DEMONSTRATORS: (Chant) Justice. Justice. Justice for all. Release Kilmar Abrego-Garcia.

The situation is tense, and violence could burst out at any moment.

GROUND REPORTER: Many years ago, one of the biggest riots burst out of a peaceful march, provoked by merciless police force trying to stop the people's march- the Rodney King riot." Today, the causes for their protest marches are rooted in social, political, and economic issues- matters of life and death. The risks are even greater.

Flashback ends.

BACK TO THE PRESENT, AT THE COURTHOUSE.

TV ANCHOR: This morning, a federal judge ruled to block Kilmar Abrego's deportation. But an hour later, the President, Gov-POT, ordered the deportation of Abrego to Uganda, defying the Judge's ruling. Well, according to the lawyers, Gov-POT has no authority to ignore or circumvent the established legal procedures- the rule of law.

The issue at hand concerns the concentration of power in the President, who is perceived to have significant influence over the actions of the three branches of government. This situation has raised concerns regarding the balance of power. Additionally, the Republican Party's alignment with the President's directives has been noted.

On the street, mixed with the protesters, a reporter interviews a group of marchers.

GROUND REPORTER: "How long have you been marching?"

MARCHER 1: Five weeks. What the government is doing is not right!"

GROUND REPORTER: What's not, right?

MARCHER 2: The government's injustice, arresting and deporting people to foreign countries, without a court hearing.

GROUND REPORTER: "What do you think may happen?

MARCHER 3: We are fed up with Gov-POT's abuse of power, like a dictator. There is no justice.

GROUND REPORTER: Do you expect a revolution?

MARCHER 1: Maybe not. Pause. But riots, strikes, and clashes with Gov-POT's forces may happen at any time.

MARCHER 3: Well, if the government pushes the people to their limit, the United States will burn.

GROUND REPORTER: You've heard the people, back to the studio.

Adam posts on social media, '*Do you want a King back?*' It is a challenging question for ordinary citizens, but they know that the American Revolution and the Declaration of Independence answered it. The people did not want to be ruled by an absolute king.

Adam and Elena's Children, Tim (Timothy) (5), a brilliant but quiet child, often asks intriguing questions and plays cops-and-robbers with Sofia (4) on the floor behind the sectional couch. They speak at the same time.

TIM: What's democracy, Dad?

SOFIA: Grampa, is democracy sick?

Startling questions, so complex that even if Elena answers, the children, perhaps, would not understand.

ELENA: Speak one at a time, ok? I'll explain that tomorrow. Now, the story is bedtime, let's go. As usual, the kids do not want to go to bed and reluctantly get up on their mother's orders.

THE NEXT DAY.

Signs of a Police State.
Mysterious drones
It's approximately 8:30 PM. A knock is heard at the door, and Robert proceeds to open it. Mrs. Ortega stands at the entrance, visibly out of breath, suggesting she may have been in a hurry.

MRS. ORTEGA: Good evening, Robert. I'm scared. (Breathe) I see outside, drones hovering like insects. They have two red eyes and move to watch us. I think people are spying on people before they take them away. How do I explain that to my students? Those insects are evil.

Elena and Adam get up and walk to greet Mrs. Ortega. She repeats her story over and over again. Mrs. Ortega is really scared.
Adam hears her comments and pays attention to their chat. They are all concerned. Her story is spooky.
They walk into the living room.

ROBERT: Flora, tell your students the government wants to watch what we are doing. (murmurs) Damn dictators!

STALKING VANTAGE VEHICLES

MRS. ORTEGA: But there is a vantage vehicle parked half a block away. Why is it there for?

ADAM: Where is that vehicle?

ELENA: She said a block away, up on our street.

MRS. ORTEGA: Excuse me, I'm so scared that I'm forgetting I brought this apple pie I baked for you.

ELENA: Thank you, Hum. Your apple pies are delicious, and with a cup of coffee, yummy! Come sit down, I'll get you a cup of tea.

Adam stealthily slips through the back door, careful to keep his footsteps light, and makes his way around the block to investigate the enigmatic vehicle that has drawn his curiosity. A sleek, black armored van, its tinted windows glistening in the faint streetlights, sits ominously parked along the curb. Perched atop the truck, a dish antenna rotates with an almost mechanical precision, its movements deliberate and calculated. Inside, a small crimson spotlight flickers to life, casting intermittent beams like a digital camera lens capturing elusive moments in the dark. With a final wary glance at the van, Adam retraces his steps along the familiar path, the soft crunch of gravel beneath his shoes the only sound breaking the stillness of the night.

At the house, the living room. They wait for Adam, curiously. Adam returns.

MARTA: What did you find out?

ADAM: Yes, it is there. They may be stalking somebody. I…

Roberts interrupts.

ROBERT: Now, I remember, I've seen school kids pasting
photos of the president on the neighborhood's lamp posts.
Gov-POT uses them. Damn narcissist dictators!

Mrs. Ortega is much calmer, joyfully chatting. She loves talking, and if let, she can chat all day long.
It is late.

MRS. ORTEGA: (yawning) Excuse me; I think I should go
home. Bring the children tomorrow, ok? Good night.

Robert and Marta walk her home. They watch the vantage vehicle still there.

Adam worries about that vantage vehicle. (He questions) Who are they after? This is the work of a dictator. He fixes his gaze on the distance, thinking.

His memories travel.

My dad possesses an impressive understanding of the intricacies of dictators' behavior. His extensive travels throughout Central America from 1980 to 2020 have allowed him to witness firsthand the actions and reigns of several notable figures. In Nicaragua, he observed Daniel Ortega, a leader whose controversial policies sparked both fervent support and fierce opposition. In Honduras, he encountered the polarizing figures of Manuel Zelaya and Juan Orlando Hernández, each leaving a distinct mark on the nation. In Guatemala, Otto Pérez Molina's tenure revealed the tumultuous relationship between governance and corruption, while in El Salvador, Salvador Sánchez Cerén's leadership illustrated the challenges of navigating a nation in transition. Lastly, he visited Panamá during the era of Ricardo Martinelli, whose administration was characterized by both economic growth and significant controversy. These experiences have given my dad a deep, nuanced perspective on the dynamics of power in the region.

They follow a standard playbook that has set rules. Anybody who observes a dictator's behavior can easily understand the dictator's pattern.

ADAM: Who can understand dictators better than my dad? The Gov-POT is an obvious wannabe dictator, as hinted by his power-grabbing attitudes.

Elena gets up from the couch.

ELENA: It's late, Adam. Let's go to bed.

Elena takes Adam's hand and tries to pull him. But no way. He is a heavy load for her. Ok, don't tell me later, I didn't call. You're going to miss it. Adam stands up, as if propelled by a strong spring, and runs after Elena.

ADAM'S PREMONITION.
A DREAM.

Around 3:30 in the morning, Adam wakes up, trembling and sweating. Elena also wakes up, awakened by the shaking bed.

ADAM: It happened again.

ELENA: The dream?

ADAM: Masked men handcuff, blindfold me, and shove me into a van.

Elena gets up, takes the pitcher of water from the bedside table, and pours a glass.

ELENA: Dear, it's just a dream. Drink some water.

ADAM: It's real! Elena, I feel it!

Adam and Elena sit on the bed for a while, embracing. After half an hour, Adam, appearing calmer, falls asleep in Elena's arms. Elena adjusts the covers around him and then returns to sleep.

The next day.

They woke up to their usual routine, and after breakfast, Adam took Tim and Sofia to the Sunshine Day Care and Pre-School. Adam engaged his children in conversation to maintain their focus.

Meanwhile, several small drones were observed flying above the neighborhood. Three or four drones, resembling insects, moved around, directing their attention toward pedestrians in the area.

Tim and Sofia look up. The drones watch them.

TIM: Those metal birds watching us; I don't like them.

SOFIA: Their eyes scare me, Dad.

ADAM: They're working, protecting us.

At the Sunshine Day Care and Pre-School, the lively sounds of children laughing and squealing fill the air as they dash around the playground, energetically playing tag. A warm breeze rustles the leaves of nearby trees, adding to the cheerful atmosphere.

At the fence gate, Mrs. Ortega stands out in her cozy slippers and soft pink nightgown, looking somewhat disheveled yet endearing. She leans down to pick up the morning newspaper from the ground, her lack of makeup revealing her natural beauty, while her tousled, unkempt hair frames her face, suggesting a relaxed morning routine.

ADAM: Good morning, Flora.

MRS. ORTEGA: Adam, don't look at me!

SOFIA: Dad, I forgot my color books. I'm sorry.

She starts crying.

ADAM: Don't worry, honey, I'll bring your books. Now, go inside. Flora, this bag of fruits is for you.

MRS. ORTEGA: (whispering) Adam (looks around), they took the Millers... last night. You, see? That's what the armored vehicle is doing. I wonder who they'll pick up next.

ADAM: And their kids?

MRS. ORTEGA: They took them too... in a different van. They left, in a hurry, in various directions.

Adams sprinted down the street, his heart pounding like a war drum in his chest. By the terrified expression etched on his face, it was clear that fear had gripped him to his very core.

Memories of the nightmare, vivid and haunting, flooded his mind as he approached his home. He threw open the door with a desperate urgency, gasping for breath as if the air itself were a lifeline.

Bursting into the living room, he felt the cool, familiar walls close in around him, yet the sense of safety was overshadowed by the lingering shadows of dread that still haunted him.

ADAM: Elena, my dream!

ELENA: It's your stress, dear, calm down.

Elena embraces Adam and gently rubs his neck. Adam, in a state of distress, returns the hug. His gaze is fixed on a space in the room.

ELENA: I'll get you water.

ADAM: Honey, it's real. I feel it. They took the Millers (pause), last night, (pause), their kids in a different vehicle.

Elena sets down the tray, causing the empty cups to fall. She observes that the situation is more serious than initially assessed.

ELENA: The Millers were distributing copies of the Constitution- that's not a crime." (She murmurs) Adam's dream is true- too many arrests in the neighborhood.

ELENA (continued): It doesn't add up. The masked men separate the terrified children from their parents, shoving the adults into one unmarked vehicle and the kids into another. What are they planning for the innocent children, and where are they taking them?

MARTA: We're going from bad to worse.

Amid his fears, Adams takes the coloring books to Sofia. But he keeps an eye on the vantage vehicle still parked on the street. The drones' eyes focus on him, following him as he changes direction.

ADAM: I don't like this... these drones move after me, looking at me. Are they after me, too?

Adam arrives at the Sunshine Day Care and Pre-Kinder facility. Mrs. Ortega, with the children, turns and walks to meet Adam at the gate.

MRS. ORTEGA: Thank you for the fruits, Adam.

ADAM: My mom, or my dad, will pick them up in the afternoon. Bye.

MRS. ORTEGA: have a good day, bye.

His mind is so preoccupied that he still holds Sofia's color book under his arm, but he turns around.

CHAPTER 2

MASKED MEN ABDUCT ADAM

ADAM IS KIDNAPPED.

Adam walks back home along the sidewalk. A black van, screeching wheels, turns to cut him off. Two aggressive masked men wearing combat gear jump off and grab him. They take and twist his arm, flipping him to the ground.

ADAM: Hey, what's this? Stop

The men strike him with brutal force, knocking him hard against the cold metal of the van. In a swift, calculated motion, they handcuff him, the sharp clink of metal echoing in the tense air. Without a moment's hesitation, they pull a black bag over his head, shrouding him in darkness and confusion. Each of their movements is precise and practiced, their training evident as they mercilessly shove him into the truck like a sack of potatoes. Within less than 30 seconds, they've executed this harrowing sequence, seamlessly orchestrated by a team of highly skilled operatives, before speeding away into the night.

Adam's world turns black, and so does his mind. He doesn't see what is going on. Flashes of his family and some good moments whirl in his mind- a possible farewell.

Elena and the family witness thekidnapping.

The sharp screech of tires pierces the stillness, snapping Robert out of his reverie on the house steps. Marta and Elena, tending to the vibrant blooms in the front garden, turn in unison, their expressions shifting from curiosity to sheer horror. Their eyes widen in disbelief as they witness the masked figures surge from a shadowy vehicle and swiftly overpower Adam. Time seems to freeze around them; their bodies become rigid, as if encased in ice. For a moment, they are paralyzed, the instinctive urge to scream caught in their throats, leaving them to choke silently on the terror that grips their hearts.

At the same time, the screeching wheels on the Pre-School front porch also draw Tim and Sofia's attention. They saw the whole flashing episode.

TIM: (screams) "Dad!"

SOFIA: "Bring my dad back, please!"

AT ADAM'S HOUSE PORCH.

Some individuals witness an abduction sequence during daylight, involving a family, including children and neighbors. The masked individuals seem unaffected by the presence of onlookers, possibly because they perceive protection from authority, leading them to believe they are invulnerable.

Elena awakens to the situation, attempts to pursue a fast-moving van, but is unable to keep up. In frustration, she kneels on the pavement, experiencing distress. Adam disappears, but the breeze flips the pages of the smashed color books lying on the pavement.

Meanwhile, Marta hurries to the daycare to retrieve the children, where conditions are chaotic, as if in an emergency. As Elena struggles to breathe, her breathing is audible, and she shows signs of denial about the unfolding events.

ELENA: (screams) "No. Not my husband, God! (murmurs)
His premonition... Is true!"

ROBERT: They won't get away with it. The people and the world will know about it. Damn dictators.

Like a wildfire, the news of the incident runs through the community. Perhaps smartphones play an important role in instant communication. But whatever it is, they rushed to the incident site to help Elena, Robert, and Marta. What just happened to Adam can happen to anybody; they know it.

Adam's Family and Neighbors react to the incident. The neighbors, surprised, scared, and concerned, quickly came to help them. They have known the Reyes family, Adam and Elena, for years.

Robert and the neighbors help Elena walk back to the porch. At the same time, more neighbors rush to support Elena and her family, showing their sincere demonstration of solidarity- and impressive action.

Those evil masked men attacked their true friends- community contributors. The masked men have no reason. It must be a sad mistake. But they immediately organize themselves, making placards and signs to display on the protest marches they start now.

News Media Broadcasts the Incident.

The piercing wail of screeching tires sends the nearby residents retreating into the safety of their homes, but this time, the cacophony is not rooted in fear. Instead, it signals the arrival of thrumming news vans and buzzing television crews, their bright logos gleaming under the dim afternoon sky as they rush to the unfolding scene. The air crackles with renewed energy as curious onlookers venture back outside, drawn by the media frenzy's magnetic pull. Reporters, armed with notepads and cameras, weave through the crowd, eagerly seeking testimonies from witnesses caught in the chaos.

Amidst the commotion, Elena stands, her heart heavy with sorrow. Tears stream down her cheeks as she grapples with the weight of her emotions. Yet, with a deep, shuddering breath, she wipes her eyes and steels herself. The grief that once threatened to overwhelm her sharpens into focus, transforming her into the resilient journalist she's always been. With a fierce glint in her eyes and unwavering determination, she steps forward, ready to uncover and convey the truth surrounding this tragic and unlawful incident.

REPORTER 1: Mrs. Reyes, why was he arrested?

REPORTER 2: Mrs. Reyes, do you know where they took Adam?

Her mind pauses for a minute, tracking the reason for Adam's abduction.

ELENA: I don't know why they arrested my husband, nor where they took him. Adam has done nothing wrong and doesn't deserve such violent treatment. Perhaps all this is a sad mistake.

More and more neighbors come to support Elena, packing the streets. Reporters are busy interviewing people. Neighbors start marching up and down the street, chanting. Bring Adam back, give him his day in court.

ROBERT: Adam is innocent. This event is an intimidation. Adam will be back.

REPORTER 1: What will your family do?

ELENA: We'll do what's legally necessary.

REPORTER 2: Will you go to CREDUM, the Civil Rights Emergency Defense Union Movement?

ELENA: Our legal strategy is confidential. The case dictates the steps we'll take, but we will follow a steady step.

Robert leans on the microphone.

ROBERT: Let's be clear. We're victims of illegal Gov-POT policies and acts. We have the right of self-defense. Damn dictators.

REPORTER 2: What do you mean by Gov-POT?

ROBERT: The Government-President of Term.

Marta takes the microphone.

MARTA: Ah! This provocative incident calls us to action: to defend and protect each other, as Lech Walesa did in Poland, or as César Chavez did in Los Angeles long ago. What happened to Adam can happen to any of you. Nobody is safe… anymore.

REPORTER 1: Provocative? What do you mean?

ROBERT: Gov-POT arrests innocent people. He wants us to react violently so he can justify his evil actions. We won't fall into his trap—damn dictators.

NEIGHBOR: We know the Reyes family for their community work, teaching Spanish, dancing, and house maintenance. They are decent people interested in the welfare of this community and this city.

As some neighbors stride purposefully along the streets, a vibrant crowd sprawls across the lush grass, the sidewalks, and the roadway that stretches out before Adam's house. Their voices create a hum of spirited energy, rising and falling like waves.

Elena and Robert step onto the porch, their expressions a mix of determination and empathy, ready to address the throng below. Meanwhile, a swarm of reporters buzzes around them, eager to grab interviews and capture the unfolding scene on camera, their equipment glinting under the sunlight.

With a sense of history hanging in the air, Elena and Robert invoke the Spirit of the 76s, their words resonating with the crowd's passion as they share the microphone, embodying a collective hope and urgency in their message.

> ELENA: This country's forefathers fought an absolute, greedy, and ruthless King and liberated the American colonies.

> ROBERT: This wannabe-king is behind Adam's abduction, and other kidnappings and deportations. Damn dictators!

> ELENA: But the spirit of 1776 still lives in our hearts. Let's form our 'Minute Neighbors' to defend and protect ourselves. Let's use our knowledge and technology as weapons to fight the invisible force behind arrests and deportations.

> ROBERT: No king, no dictator like those in Central America. No, we will not let them get away with this.

NEIGHBORS SOLIDARITY.

> Street in Front of Adam's House.
> A drumbeat sound plays in the background. The crowd, now more organized, marches in the street while chanting.

> CROWD: Et Pluribus Unum, Et Pluribus Unum, Et Pluribus Unum. We, the people, united, cannot be blighted.

> ELENA: We, law-abiding citizens, can't succumb. We'll protest peacefully and lawfully. We'll stand our ground together, *"all for one and one for all."*

> ROBERT: Intimidation! That's the continuous action of a dictator. And if he succeeds, he can then do anything he wants—damn dictators.

In the background, a dramatic drumbeat persists, in sync with their heartbeat as they march, reflecting anger, frustration, and grief.

> NEIGHBORS: (Chant) Unite, unite, unite. The people united cannot be blighted. Unite your force with ours. Unite for just one cause. Unite to have a better life.

The marches continue consistently, occurring every day at all hours. This activity is increasingly integrated into participants' daily routines, as they attend work, manage personal responsibilities, and engage in marches.

LEGAL SUPPORT DROPS FROM THE VOID.
DEFENSIVE REACTIONS

IN ELENA'S HOUSE, LIVING ROOM. DAY.

The day remains bright and clear, casting a warm glow through the windows of Adam's cozy living room. Inside, Elena, Robert, and several community leaders are gathered for an urgent meeting, their expressions serious as they discuss matters that weigh heavily on their minds—far removed from the innocent tales usually told to children. Meanwhile, Marta gently guides the kids to the playroom, where the sounds of laughter and playful chatter contrast sharply with the gravity of the adults' conversation.

> ELENA: Oppression, exploitation, and repression have been the history of humanity: greedy over needy. We must not allow the rise of another king or a dictator in the United States. Not now, not ever.

THE LEGAL AID.

Robert finishes typing and starts printing a document—phone rings. Everybody jumps, startled. JUSTIN MORALES, a young lawyer in his 30s, calls Elena. Elena, as she finishes speaking, answers.

ELENA: Hello, this is she. Hold on, Mr. Morales, I'll put you on speakers. (Pause) Go ahead.

JUSTIN (V.O.): Mrs. Reyes, you may call me Justin. CREDUM assigns me to Adam's case. May I come to see you in 20-30 minutes?

ELENA: (excited) Yes, of course, Justin. We'll wait for you.

The call ends. She jumps, overjoyed, and screams.
ELENA: WE GOT A LAWYER!

Family, community leaders, and neighbors, rise, instantly, with a solid scream, 'JUSTICE WILL COME.' Now, they feel that hope may come, even in the most adverse situation- there is hope.

Outside on the street, in front of the Reyes' house. The sun suddenly brightens. The marchers scream, 'E Pluribus Unum' JUSTICE FOR ALL.' They continue marching and chanting slogans.

The dramatic drum keeps sounding in the background, and its beats make the march even more impressive and awesome.

CROWD:(Chant) We, the people united, cannot be blighted. Unite, unite, unite. Unite your force with ours. Unite for just one cause. Unite for a better life. Bring Adam back.

THE MATCH- REYES VS. GOV-POT.
IN AN UNKNOWN COUNTRY'S PRISON.

Adam is in a six-by-four-foot cell, no windows, no bed, no toilet. A dim light comes through the barred door viewport.
ADAM: (whispers) ELENA, hear my thoughts; recall our chats; lead the people to resist.

BACK IN ADAM'S HOUSE, LIVING ROOM.

Surprised, her eyes widened, and her face lit up; a thought darted into Elenas' mind. She whispers.

> ELENA: Adam, your character, strength, and thoughts guide our actions, prudently and swiftly, as you would do it.

> ROBERT: Let's fight the wannabe-king, as in the mid 1770's. for our liberty.

> ELENA: Freedom for us is crucial to save Adam and our democracy.

The community leaders are shocked. Marta comes back.

> MARTA: Immigrants created this government, and our Constitution describes it as a democratic republic- No kings, no dictators.

FIFTEEN MINUTES LATER.

Justin, tall, elegantly dressed in a blue suit and red tie, arrives with a briefcase under his arm. He sees Elena. (Private point of view, POV) Wow, what a beautiful woman. Elena notices his look and, embarrassed, lowers her head. But indeed, she is beautiful, a model with qualifications.

> JUSTIN: Mrs. Reyes, Adam's whereabouts are unknown. The government says Adam Reyes is not in their records and denies any involvement in his arrest.

IN A REMOTE TORTURE SITE.

In a dimly lit, abandoned manufacturing facility, a sense of foreboding hangs heavily in the stale air. Adam finds himself suspended, his wrists bound tightly above him, helplessly dangling from an old, rusted roof beam. The sharp bite of the chains that anchor his ankles to the cold concrete floor keeps him painfully stretched out, a grim reminder of his precarious situation.

Surrounding him are four masked figures, their movements swift and deliberate, cloaked in shadow. Each man grips a metal chain wrapped in a layer of rubber hose, a cruel instrument designed to inflict maximum pain while minimizing visible damage. As they interrogate him, their voices are low but menacing, demanding answers that Adam doesn't possess.

With every crack of the chain against his skin, the metal bites through his flesh, leaving cruel welts and bruises in its wake. Confusion and terror swirl in Adam's mind, robbing him of coherence as he struggles to comprehend the nature of their questions. Time blurs as he balances on the precipice of consciousness, desperate to hold onto his sanity.

But the relentless torment takes its toll. The world grows darker and more distant, and just as he feels himself slipping away, the interrogation abruptly ceases. The masked men exchange glances, their expressions obscured, leaving a chilling silence that fills the room as Adam succumbs to the void of unconsciousness.

AT THIS HOUSE LIVING ROOM.

> ROBERT: LIARS! The Gov-POT is making our country like Nicaragua, Venezuela, or Russia... Damn Dictators.

> JUSTIN: We introduced a writ of Habeas corpus petition and a motion to present charges in court.

> ELENA: (sobbing) Can we see him?

> JUSTIN: We'll see Adam after the court assumes his custody in a local secure detention facility.

Justin keeps looking at Elena, who is embellished. He turns, shakes his head, and leaves.

MARTA: (crying) My son is not a criminal!

ROBERT: Gov-POT intimidates people, steals, eliminates their opponents, and then says he doesn't know anything about it.

CRUEL INTIMIDATION.

In the dim light of the secret prison, the air feels thick with despair. Adam paces the cold, hard floor, his movements restless and agitated, much like a caged Bengal tiger. The walls bear the marks of his turmoil, scratched and scuffed as if his very frustration is clawing at the unforgiving surfaces. He often pauses to press his palms against the rough stone, staring blankly as he delves deep into his own heart, tearing through layers of anguish in a desperate quest for liberation. The weight of his innocence hangs heavy on his shoulders, a painful reminder of the freedom he yearns for, a freedom that feels just out of reach.

ADAM: Oh God! I can resist, but not for long. Let me know what Elena and my dad are doing. Let me help them!

Adam is lost, helpless, his world reduced to a twenty-four-square-foot floor. He can barely move or convert his thoughts into significant actions.

IN ADAM'S HOUSE.

Elena finishes her meeting with family and community leaders.

ELENA: So, this is our organization- the People for the People movement, PFP.

The *'people for the people movement.'* This is the people's commitment, similar to the Minute Man organization during the 1776

American Revolution, designed by the people to protect and defend the people against unscrupulous attacks by the king of England.

ROBERT: And this is our strategic plan.

Robert hands out stacks of booklets to community leaders, as they leave- The cover reads, "Resistance Plan of Action (RPA).
At the Masked Men hide out.
The phone rings, and the leader answers.

Masked men Leader: Yes, Boss, when? Ok. I understand. We'll do.

Three days later.

Threats to Elena and her family.

TV ANCHOR: **Breaking News!** We have been informed that unknown agents have orders to hurt Adam Reyes' family if they don't stop instigating the people.

People on the streets and neighbors always find out what's going on with the PFP movement.

The neighbors, deeply moved by the tragic news, poured out onto the streets to stand in solidarity with the Reyes family. Concerned faces, filled with empathy and sorrow, filled the surrounding area as they gathered to show their support. News radio and television crews surged toward the scene, their cameras whirring and microphones poised, eager to capture the unfolding story and the raw emotions of the moment.

Amidst the murmurs of the crowd, Elena, Robert, and Marta stepped forward, their hearts heavy with grief yet determined to face the throng of reporters and onlookers. The air was thick with anticipation, the rustle of notes and chatter mingling with the whispers of the heartbreak that had struck their community. Together, the three of them stood strong, gazing out at the sea of sympathetic faces that surrounded them.

REPORTER 1 (V.O.): Mrs. Reyes, is it faithful you and your family received death threats?

REPORTER 2 (V.O.): Who threatened you, the government?

ELENA: Yes, we received an anonymous envelope and phone calls. We don't know the sources.

REPORTER 1 (V.O.): Can you share the threatening documents?

REPORTER 2 (V.O.): Did you record the phone calls?

ELENA: No. This evidence is in the hands of the authorities, our private investigator, and our lawyer.

Elena knows this information is critical and private, part of a legal case.

ROBERT: In countries like Nicaragua, dictators use the same playbook while staying in the shadows.

Gov-POT embodies the very essence of a wannabe dictator—his demeanor suggests an authoritarian presence, his rhetoric drips with oppressive undertones, and his actions reflect a blatant disregard for democratic principles. However, the situation is even more alarming. He appears to be emulating the darkest chapters of history, reminiscent of Hitler's horrific Holocaust, as he orchestrates the arrest and deportation of individuals based solely on their race or for merely opposing him. This is not just a violation of human rights; it constitutes a chilling act of racial cleansing, systemic discrimination, and the ruthless elimination of those he perceives as adversaries.

AGENTS TORTURE ADAM.

A red phone rings on the warden's desk.

> Warden: Hello, sir, at your command. Yes, sir, I understand.
> We'll get him sick… (pause) we'll proceed.

In the dimly lit confines of the secret prison cell, the agents intensified their cruel methods of torture against Adam. They withheld both water and food, leaving him with a gnawing hunger and parched throat. To further torment him, they subjected him to a relentless barrage of startling noises, shattering the silence of his confinement and preventing even the slightest chance of sleep.

The air in the cell grew heavy with despair as the agents deliberately neglected the filth accumulating around him, allowing the makeshift toilet to overflow and fester. Each moment stretched into an eternity, as Adam grappled with the physical and psychological torment designed to break his spirit.

> ADAMS (POV): This torture-surge must be a government's reaction to my family's resistance. They must be fighting hard, Gov-POT.

AT THE UNKNOWN PRIESO. THREE DAYS LATER

Torturers tower around Adam, their menacing presence casting a dark shadow over him. They thrust a phone into his trembling hands, the cold plastic a stark reminder of his grim reality. With a knot tightening in his stomach, Adam understands the cruel ultimatum: comply, or face further torment.

Each second drags painfully as he weighs his options, a palpable fear coursing through him. He lets out a defeated moan, stalling for time, yet the threat of their relentless beating looms over him like a storm cloud. Finally, with a heavy heart, he dials his home number, longing for the safety and warmth of Los Angeles, knowing that his only chance to end the torture lies in this one agonizing call.

AT ELENA'S HOUSE LIVING ROOM.

The telephone rings. Elena jumps to answer. The call is from an unknown number.
At Adam's home in Los Angeles.

The phone rings. Elena answers.

ELENA: Hello, this is Elena. Hello.

AT THE UNKNOWN PRISON.

ADAM (V.O.): It's me, Adam... breathe (pause).

Elena covers the phone and screams (V.O.) IT'S ADAM!!

ELENA: ADAM! (sobbing) Are you ok? Where do they keep you?

Adam is tired, breathing hard, and almost fainting. His overwhelming joy ties his throat in a lump. He waits, looking around at his torturers.
A torturer points a gun at his head and gestures for him not to answer any questions. Adam doesn't answer.

ADAM (V.O.): Please, do not oppose the government.

Adam is beaten, thirsty, hungry, and sleepy. The torturers shut off the phone.

AT ELENA'S HOUSE LIVING ROOM.

ELENA: Hello, Adam, hello…

There's a long beep on the phone.

ROBERT: Damn, they cut off the phone. Hang up. The torturers control this call.

Elena and Marta cry, embracing each other. Images of Adam being tortured rush to their minds. The mixed emotions of joy, fear, and grief swirl in their heart.

ROBERT: I got it!

MARTA: My innocent Adam...

ELENA: Robert, call Justin and Sherlock.

Marta, still sobbing, grieving, brings warm tea.
An hour later.
The telephone rings. Elena answers.

JUSTIN (O.S.): Mrs. Reyes, I can't come. Please save that call recording...

ROBERT: Damn!

ELENA: Darn! When we need to get in touch with someone...

Door knocks. Robert greets SHERLOCK, a private investigator, in his mid-40s, dressed as a construction worker. After listening to the recording several times.

SHERLOCK: Hum! I have no doubts. This is a coded phone call. As weak as Adam is, he framed his message perfectly.

ROBERT: Explain it, please.

ELENA: What does he say?

SHERLOCK: He fluently self-identifies himself, "It's me, Adam. Waits for that to think. Then, clearly says, "Please do," pauses; he softly says, "not," and then, a bit louder, says, oppose, (quickly accents), the government.

MARTA: So, what's the message?

SHERLOCK: **"Please, do** not **oppose the government."** Very clever, no?

Sherlock tries to trace the phone call's origin, but there isn't enough time.

The telephone rings. Robert answers and places the phone on the speakers.

ROBERT: This is Robert.

JUSTIN (V.O.): Robert, please give that evidence to Sherlock. I'll meet him this evening. Thank you.

Sherlock leaves. Elena wipes the tear from her face, sighs, shakes her head, and takes leadership. She walks to the house porch. News reporters run to meet her, Marta, and Robert. The crowd on the porch stands behind the reporters.

REPORTER 1: We understand you just talked to your husband?

REPORTER 2: Has he been torture, how is he?

ELENA: Yes, we talked to Adam, and yes, he has been tortured and forced to call us.

REPORTER 2: Can you tell us what you talked about?

ELENA: Their torturers forced him to tell us to stop marches protesting his abduction. We assume that our marches are effectively impacting the Gov-POT dictatorial action plans.

REPORTER 1: What will you and your family do?

Elena calls on Robert to answer.

ROBERT: There's nothing we can do; protest marches are spread all over the nation- (pause) out of our control.

ELENA: Adam's legal cases are pending in various courts. We can't stop these proceedings. They are out of our hands.

OUTSIDE ON THE STREETS.

The throngs of people pour into the streets, their marches and demonstrations growing more fervent and resolute by the hour. Stopping now is not an option; a passionate fire has ignited within them. Their anger is a powerful force, fueled not only by the shocking abduction of Adam but also by a tide of similar injustices that have swept across the nation like a dark shadow. It's no longer just an isolated incident—it's the spark that has set off a national movement, a clarion call for justice: **People for the People**. The spirit of unity and determination pulses through the crowd, echoing their demand for change and accountability, as they raise their voices in unison against oppression.

THE RESISTANCE INTENSIFIES.

ELENA: This is not an isolated event; it is a Gov-POT national wave of hate, a racial cleansing plan to make

America white again. Gov-POT is following Adolf Hitler's path, when he killed around six million Jews- a genocide.

ROBERT: But we have learned that when the people resist and fight back, the government cannot do what it wants.

Elena refuses to back down; she chooses to fight back. And while she discusses it with Robert and community leaders from a distance, her body language and gestures suggest she is instructing them on how to execute their marchers.

Sometimes, when conditions and situations darken our environment, light comes up from nowhere, and a spot shines where we stand. It appears that existence balances situations and circumstances to create a fair world.

Elena returns to journalism.

The sequence of events takes an unexpected turn. It is as if superior forces are trying to put the opposing forces on equal terms, benefiting the Reyes family.

The telephone rings. Marta answers.

MARTA: Hello, this is Marta. Oh yes, wait a minute.

Elena is outside with the community, leaders, and the crowd. Marta walks to the front door and calls Elena.

ELENA: This is Elena. Oh! What a surprise. What's going on? (Pause) Really! (Pause) Yes, of course… When? (Pause) Ok, I'll let you know my decision tomorrow… yes, bye.

Elena hangs up and goes back inside.

ELENA: Wow. They want me back right away. (She shouts) Robert, Marta, come.

Elena discusses the job offer she got from her former employer, P-TV-N, with Robert and Marta.

> ROBERT: It is a great opportunity to support Adam's legal case, and you'll have data access, resources, and journalists' protection.

> MARTA: Tim and Sofia are older. Robert and I can take care of them. Take the P-TV-N's job.

If people observed life, they would probably see that an event occurs for a reason, according to the causes that bring it about. But the effect is positive or negative, depending on personal attitudes and interpretations of the result. Elena examines the factors that have contributed to her success. She takes the P-TV-N job.

People's march grows.

On Adam's house street, the dramatic drumbeat sounds louder in the background, and the people march, chanting to calm their frustrations and fears.

> CROWD: (lead) We, the people, united, cannot be blighted. (chorus) Et Pluribus Unum. (lead) Unite your force with ours. (chorus) Et Pluribus Unum. (lead) Unite for just one cause. (chorus) Et Pluribus Unum. (lead) Unite to lead a better life. (chorus) Et Pluribus Unum.

The marchers pound their feet against the pavement, each syllable of the word "Et" resonating like a call to arms. They move with the precision and discipline of a well-trained battalion in a grand parade, their synchronized steps echoing their resolute message. Their movements serve one singular purpose: to express their unwavering rejection of an authoritarian regime that stifles their freedoms, constricts their way of life, and undermines their right to exist as dignified human beings.

This nation—its vast territory and abundant natural resources—rightfully belongs to its people and their future generations, equally. The government, in all its forms and functions, is theirs to shape and direct. The Constitution, a carefully crafted document for the people, serves as a thorough guide outlining the principles and rules by which they desire their nation to be governed.

We, the people, firmly assert that on election day, we do not relinquish our rights to what rightfully belongs to us—this cherished nation. We do not cast our ballots to appoint a king or a dictator to preside over us. Never.

CHAPTER 3

VIOLENT
PERSECUTIONS INCREASE

FIVE DAYS LATER

On a bright afternoon, a chain of actions reveals the government's escalation of violence and rudeness; for instance, the marches outside Elena's house. Elena returns from work as Mrs. Ortega arrives at the house.

MRS. ORTEGA: Elena, coincidence. How's work?

ELENA: Exciting and happy. The best, I can speak loud and clear. I can also work from home. How are you?

MRS. ORTEGA: Fine, I'm so glad you talked to Adam. He is so brave, well, all of you are so. Ah. I brought you this pot of beef-and-veggies soup.

ELENA: Thank you, Flora. Hum. It smells so good.

Elena and Marta walk to the kitchen, chatting. Mrs. Ortega kept talking to Robert.

MARTA (V.O.): Flora (Mrs. Ortega), would you like tea?

MRS. ORTEGA: Oh yes, thank you... Robert, four masked men took the Fonseca family and their teenagers this afternoon. Ryan was in my day care, so I'm keeping him.

ROBERT: Flora, you're Ryan's legal guardian, from the time they bring him to you until they pick him up. You hold a child care and teaching preschool agreement, signed and dated by his parents, that frames the custody time.

Elena comes back to the living room with tea and cups.

ELENA: That's right, Flora: only Ryan's parents, and or their authorized person, can pick him up. That's the law.

MRS. ORTEGA: This situation is terrible. Shall I report it to the police and media?

ELENA: Not before 72 hours. The police can't do anything until then. (pause) I'll send a news crew tomorrow morning for an interview. That's a way to make this incident public while you exercise your legal responsibility.

Mrs. Ortega, confident and reassured, leaves. Robert and Marta escort her back to her home.
In an unknown quarter.
Agents act according to the instructions they received from their remote boss. The phone rings. Their leader answers.

AGENT LEADER: Yes, sir, we are. We can do that tonight, past midnight. Yes, sir, no tracks, we understand.

Elena's home is vandalized.
The following morning, as usual, Marta gets up early to make breakfast. She walks to the living room, turns the lights on and...

MARTA: (scream) Oh, my God! **Robert, we've been robbed!**

Robert, already up, runs. Elena wakes up and runs. The living room is a mess. Binders and folders emptied, books from the shelves, and documents on the floor. Drawers are open and searched. Two laptops are crashed on the floor. They check; nothing is missing. Marta walks to pick up books.

ROBERT: Marta, don't touch anything!

Elena calls Sherlock. Robert thinks the house had been bugged, with hidden cameras and mics.

ROBERT: We need pest and bug control.

Robert casually points his eyes and ears, as if it were a personal body code. Twenty minutes later, A P-TV-N news crew arrives and starts taking footage of the scene and interviewing Elena and family.

P-TV-N REPORTER: Mrs. Reyes, who vandalized your house?

REPORTER 1: What were they looking for?

REPORTER 2: Is it a government intimidation tactic?

ELENA: One question at a time, guys, please. We don't know who; they may be looking for incriminating papers. (pause) Please don't step on, touch, or disturb the evidence. We need it to preserve what the vandals left for our investigator and lawyer.

ROBERT: Yes, it looks like a dictator's threatening action to silence us.

P-TV-N REPORTER: Have you called your investigator?

ROBERT: No, but we're preserving the evidence for him to examine.

REPORTER 2: You work for P-TV-N. Does this have anything to do with it?

She stops to think, then looks down, hand over her mouth. Elena (POV): Silently, she exposes that 'Yes, of course, I'm a Gov-POT journalist threat." She looks up, straight-faced, positive.

ELENA: No, the vandalism in this private property by unknown characters is news P-TV-N can report.

ROBERT: Everything goes from cause to effect, and Adam's case goes from provocation to consequences.

Obviously, Robert refers to Gov-POT's abuse of power, stepping over the rule of law, and citizens' rights.

About an hour later, Sherlock arrives, inspects the scene, stands, and holds his chin, moving his eyes from side to side.

SHERLOCK: Mrs. Reyes, this is a professional job. There are no tracks. It was perfectly executed. Ha, the alarm was set off. The surveillance cameras were inactive. I'm puzzled; how did they break in?

Sherlock pulls a chair to face the crime scene and scans the space from point to point.

Meanwhile, at the Day Care, Pre School front porch, a reporting team from P-TV-N arrives at Safe Heaven Day Care and Kindergarten around 8:30 a.m. to interview Mrs. Ortega.

P-TV-N REPORTER: Mrs. Ortega, you're keeping Ryan Fonseca, five, in your custody. Can you tell us why?

The camera crew focuses on Ryan, who stands next to Mrs. Ortega, holding her hand, not really aware of his situation, but he is grieving, sad, and missing his parents.

Mrs. Ortega becomes emotional, sobbing, her tears roll down her aging cheeks. It's not easy; the psychological burden is too heavy for her ailing heart. But she hopes this incident does not end in an irreparable event. She waits for her lump in her throat to fade out.

MRS. ORTEGA: Yesterday, I heard screaming and crying in the house behind mine... From my second floor, overlooking my neighbor's house driveway, I saw armed masked men taking the Fonseca away. Ryan was with me, and so they did take him. Perhaps they did not even know about him. I'm not good at taking videos with my digital camera, but I recorded the incident.

P-TV-N REPORTER: Are you legally responsible for keeping Ryan?

MRS. ORTEGA: Yes, I have signed a custodial agreement with Ryan's parents and me, stating that I can only release their child to their parents or an authorized person.

P-TV-N REPORTER: Mrs. Ortega, congratulations! You're doing an excellent service, thank you for this interview. Our channel will air this interview as soon as possible.

Air Reporters.

A P-TV-N news helicopter hovers over Elena's house. On the street, more and more enraged neighbors join the march as it goes up and down. The persistent, dramatic drumbeat sounds steadily in the background.

NEIGHBORS: (lead) Et Pluribus Unum. (Chorus) Unite, unite, unite. (lead) Unite your force with ours. (lead) Unite for just one cause. Unite for freedom and peace. Unite, unite, unite.

Adam's children were harassed.

At the Day Care – Pre School, children play in the front playground, happily, unconcerned with socio-political-economic problems- they are innocent, not knowing the perils of life. A man wearing dark glasses stands by the fence, calling Tim and Sofia. The children start walking towards the man.

Fortunately, Mrs. Ortega, who has been watching from the window, comes out and calls Tim and Sofia. The man walks away. Mrs. Ortega watched him walk hurriedly to a black van parked half a block away. The van drives away. She saved Adam's children.

Situations and conditions in life do not come isolated; they are constantly appearing interconnected or tied with other situations and conditions, like a fishing net- a matrix. Each knot is an event, and the strings leading to the knots are the path that situations and conditions weave. A Sequence of events quickly evolves.

In the living room at Adam's house, Robert and Marta work with the community leaders.

The phone rings. Marta answers, placing the call on speakers.

MARTA: Hello, Marta speaking.

JUSTIN (V.O.): Excuse me, Mrs. Reyes, I forgot Elena is at P-TV-N. Please tell her and Robert that Adam's court hearing starts in 30 minutes. It may last two hours. But today the government must present its evidence.

ROBERT: Hi, Justin. This is Robert. I'm listening. We'll do. Thank you. I'll record so Elena can watch it later.

Two and a Half hours later, at the Court. They all rise, and the judge sits at the bench. They all sit.

THE JUDGE: In the matter of the Government vs. Adam Reyes, this Court orders the government to bring Adam back to the US within five days and formally charge him within thirty days.

Robert shakes his head in disbelief, but he gets excited anyway.

Robert and Marta, along with some neighbors in the living room, jumped and screamed, "Justice for all."

ON THE STREET, IN FRONT OF ADAM'S HOUSE. DAY.

The news filtered to the people. Cheers broke the suspense, the people danced, and continued the march up and down the street with greater energy.

Robert distrusts Gov-POT compliance.

INSIDE ELENA'S HOUSE, LIVING ROOM. SAME DAY.

ROBERT: I predict the government will ignore this ruling and attempt to delay the proceedings by using the dictator's playbook.

Dictator's Playbook Explained.

LEADERS: Would you please explain the playbook?

Elena comes back from work, but in time, listens to the last comment.

ELENA: The wannabe dictator beginning his learning curve is unpredictable and dangerous.

ROBERT: To understand it better, let's play the game of dictators' playbook rules. I'll recite a rule, and you find an example. Rule 1: Create chaos and confusion.

A LEADER: Right! He scrambles the national economy- the tariffs that affect our small businesses.

ROBERT: Rule 2: Divide and conquer.

MARTA: Yes, He creates racial conflicts and then blames the government's problems on his adversaries.

ROBERT: Rule 3: Tests his power limits.

ELENA: Of course, he defies the rule of law, claiming unawareness and innocence, and holding his actions valid and enforceable.

ROBERT: Rule 4: Break the rule of law.

MRS. ORTEGA ARRIVES WITH A PUDDING AND, FROM THE DOOR, ANSWERS.

MRS. ORTEGA: ¡Aha! He says the justice system is ineffective and claims absolute power and total immunity.
Elena takes the booklet, while Robert steps out for a moment.

ELENA: Rule 5: Promise deportation by millions per month.

Top leader: He looks for statistical numbers, not criminals, as he promised, and blames the nation for problems with racial population components.

ELENA: Rule 6: Place himself above the law.

MARTA: He arrests and deports innocent working people, calling them criminals without due process of law.

There is silence, Robert returns, raising his arm. Elena gestures 'go ahead.

ROBERT: He thinks he is the law and eliminates justice, denying people's right to due process in court. Damn dictators.

So, the leaders got a manual of the dictator's playbook rules. The community leaders leave, ready to go to work.

Telephone ring. Marta answers.

MARTA
Hello, this is Marta... yes... (to Elena) Elena, it's for you.

DETECTIVE INVESTIGATION.
SHERLOCK (V.O.): Mrs. Reyes, I'm positive that the vandals cut the power circuit grid serving your house. They used secret service tools to open the front door after shutting off the electricity. I already informed Justin.

ROBERT: Do we need to change security devices?

SHERLOCK (V.O.): None. They won't be back. They got what they wanted.

GOVERNMENT'S DECEIVING ACTIONS.
BACK AT ELENA'S HOUSE, LIVING ROOM, IN THE DAYTIME.

The living room looks like a situation room: an oval meeting table full of papers, documents, and law books; the wall-mounted TV is on, tuned to P-TV-N (Popular Television Network).

Elena (POV): (with wandering eyes) I need to call Justin. (pause) I need to know what he is doing.

SHOWING ON THE TV

TV ANCHOR: Yesterday, the Attorney General said the president's enemies instigate the people's marches, feeding people fake theories against him.

ROBERT: Shame on them. Damn dictators!

Marta brings a tray with a coffee pot and cups.

MARTA: Aha! Orchestrated lies. Coffee anyone?

ELENA: He pleases himself, eliminating anyone or whomever in his way.

ON THE TV.

TV ANCHOR: **Breaking News!** This morning, the president ordered the arrest of instigators who discredit him, demeaning his beautiful, never-before-done deals. He says journalists are the enemies of the people and...

The Anchor stops, steps off screen. A commercial comes on. A couple of minutes later...
At the Los Angeles Federal building.

LIVE TV VIDEO:

A United States Senator posed several questions to the Homeland Security Secretary. Civilian men and FBI agents violently grab the Senator, slam him to the floor, throw him to the ground, handcuff him, lift him up, forcibly remove him from the room, and take him away through the halls to another room.

TV ANCHOR: American citizens have not seen such an abuse of power by any past government in the two hundred years of American democracy.

ROBERT: Gov-POT is crossing the ultimate line. He places himself above the rule of law and the Constitution. Damn dictators.

A large crowd in Los Angeles has been marching in protest of Gov-POT's order to crack down on public demonstrations.

WHITE HOUSE, NEWS ROOM. DAY

SECRETARY OF STATE: "The president has nothing to do with the incident. Because he loves and obeys the rule of law, he has ordered an immediate investigation."

Back at Elena's house, living room, same day.

ROBERT: Liars! Damn dictators.

ELENA: The Truth will come out... Soon!

On THE STREET, FRONT OF ADAM'S HOUSE. DAY.

People, reacting furiously, march up and down the street. The persistent, dramatic drumbeat sounds in the background.

CROWD: (Lead) We, the people, united, cannot be blighted. (chorus) Et Pluribus Unum. (lead) Unite your force with ours. (chorus) Et Pluribus Unum. (lead) Unite for just one cause. (chorus) Et Pluribus Unum. (lead) Unite to lead a better life.

They stomp the floor each time they say the word "ET." Community leaders approach Elena and Robert, standing on the porch.

IN ELENA'S HOUSE, LIVING ROOM.

ELENA: This isn't what the people fought for in 1776 – This abuse of power is clearly the whim of a wannabe-king.

MARTA: Cruel, egotistical.

ROBERT: A dictator in action. Damn dictators.

Tim and Sofia are playing behind the sectional couch, trying to understand the words in the adults' conversation.

TIM: Mom, what's a dictator? Is it an alligator?

SOFIA: Is that why they are so cruel, Mom?

Elena gestures for Marta to take the children to their playroom.

IN JUSTIN'S OFFICE, SAME DAY.

Shuffling documents, he stops...
JUSTIN (POV.): What beautiful woman, (pause) grieving this big mess.
ALL IS LOST.

BACK IN ELENA'S HOUSE, LIVING ROOM.

Elena, Robert, and community leaders hurriedly work on strategies. Phone ring. Elena answers.

JUSTIN (V.O.)
Mrs. Reyes, the Supreme Court ruled Gov-POT may arrest
and deport criminals to any prison, domestic or foreign.
CREDUM ended our work.

The news fell on them like a bucket of ice water. They stop working. They look at each other in great surprise, wondering about what to do next.

ROBERT: By granting Gov-POT such power, the Supreme
Court officially established a dictatorship in this country.
They place the President above the law.

MARTA: Oh God, please, save my son, save this country.

Elena drops to her knees, arms up to the sky, and Marta faints. Community leaders, eyes and mouths open, scream, "OH, NO!" Tim and Sofia scream and cry, even though they do not know what is happening. They run to their mom, scared.

SOFIA: Dad, come back.

TIM: We'll wait for you, Dad.

ROBERT: We lost it all! We can't save Adam. Damn dictators! We lost our liberties, our rights, our democracy, our country!

Silence takes over the room.
FADE TO BLACK.

CHAPTER 4

POINT OF NO RETURN

Commitment to Resist.

IN ELENA'S HOUSE, LIVING ROOM. DAY, 3:00 P.M.

The ambient is gloomy and quiet, secluded. The curtains are down, closing the windows. No lights in the living room. The TV is off. Marta and Robert sit on the couch, in silence. Elena, elbows on knees, holds her head, sadly grieving. Robert's eyes closed, fixed gaze on the ceiling as if thinking. Marta helps the children with their homework. The world and life have ended for them.

Elena screams!

ELENA: NOT TRUE! THIS CASE IS NOT OVER. (sobs) We'll win. He'll come back, (Pause) We're not giving up. Not now, NEVER!

MARTA: My son is innocent!

Elena slumps back on the couch, mumbling. Robert, admiring her courage, turns to Elena.

Door knock. Marta opens. Mrs. Ortega comes in, carrying a pot.

MRS. ORTEGA: Elena, your children didn't come to school today; I thought...

Elena cries, leaning onto Mrs. Ortega.

ELENA (CRYING): Don't say it, Flora, don't say it.

Elena and Marta get emotional as they grieve.

MRS. ORTEGA: I heard your screams at the door. What's going on? You all look down! May I help you with something? Pause.

Elena, overwhelmed by a tide of emotions and shrouded in a haze of grief, stepped forward and enveloped Mrs. Ortega in a heartfelt embrace. Tears glimmered in her eyes as she clung tightly, seeking solace in the warmth of another's presence amid the swirling uncertainties that surrounded her.

ELENA: Flora, our life has come to a stop-the government... (sobs) We can't fight its power. He controls the three branches of our government.

Mrs. Ortega looks puzzled, trying to make sense of what Elena says. Robert, looking at Mrs. Ortega, steps and leads her to the living room.

ROBERT: Flora, the Supreme Court enables Gov-POT to arrest and deport anyone he deems criminal.

MRS. ORTEGA: That's upsetting her. In her case, I'd be upset too-well, more than that.
Elena jumps like catapulted by a spring.

ELENA: (Screams) **I'll fight to my last breath to bring Adam back.** (pause) The kids need their dad, and I need my husband. (Screams) **This is our point of no return.** (pause) As Patrick Henry said once (quotes), "*Give me liberty or give me death.*"

Robert hugs Elena, comforting her. Marta and Mrs. Ortega walk off to the kitchen. The children play behind the couch.

Mrs. Ortega brings back a cup of tea and an anti-anxiety pill for Elena.

MRS. ORTEGA: Here, dear, take this pill and tea. You'll feel better.

MINUTES LATER.

SOFIA: (sobbing) Mom, Dad's not coming back, (pause) ever?

TIM: Don't say that! My Dad will come back. You'll see.

ELENA: It isn't that dear. He'll be back, but it may take time.

The community leaders arrived in a flurry, their footsteps echoing through the bustling house. Robert, with a warm smile, welcomed them at the door, setting a tone of camaraderie. In the kitchen, the tantalizing aroma of simmering soup wafted through the air as Mrs. Ortega and Marta efficiently ladled hearty servings into bowls, ensuring everyone was taken care of.

Meanwhile, Elena and her family busily prepared for the day ahead, their movements choreographed like a well-rehearsed dance. The living room buzzed with energy; its surfaces cluttered with tools and materials that hinted at a continuous flurry of activity. It was clear they had been working tirelessly for what felt like a month, and yet, despite the chaos around them, there was an unmistakable sense of purpose. They worked with a sense of urgency, every action reflecting the pressure of being behind schedule, yet united in their determination.

Mrs. Ortega leaves.

ROBERT: Ok. Let's have our meeting.

On the table.

A list of Gov-POT's donors and supporters, including billionaires and millionaires, top principal names, business addresses, and phone numbers, lies on the table.

> ELENA: We'll make our marches engaging, more expressive, and effective. We'll reduce, eliminate, and prevent big Gov-POT's donors and enablers: fixers and doers. These enablers, fixers, and doers are the real enemies of the people.

Indeed, anything without needed support will fall, and that is true. After long hours of discussion, they came up with a plan. The meeting ends. Community leaders leave to implement their strategy.

People react to Gov-POT's abuse of power.

A news helicopter hovers over down town Los Angeles. Day time.

A P-TV-N air news crew hovers over downtown Los Angeles. Reporters estimate over 100,000 people march through the streets, circling around the federal court. Five hundred Marines occupy downtown Los Angeles, under Gov-POT's order. The people ignore them, but the guards and marines, with their arms ready, are positioned around the courthouse.

> P-TV-N REPORTER: We have never seen military troops on any US city streets. But is it legal to deploy soldiers to US cities?

The Constitution says this is not legal; it's an issue that will be vented in US courts, sooner or later.

AT THE STATE CAPITOL, SACRAMENTO, CA. toDAY

In a news conference in front of the building, the Governor challenges the President's order to federalize the National Guard and mobilize Marine soldiers to the city of Los Angeles.

P-TV-N REPORTER: **BREAKING NEWS!** The Governor of California pleads with the people to remain calm when facing military forces. The president's actions are unconstitutional, and we'll take legal action in court.

OUTSIDE ADAM REYES HOUSE.

The day is overcast; dark clouds drift above; there's no sun. Drones float over; the vantage vehicle is still parked on the neighborhood's street. The people march up and down, chanting their slogans.

At the same time, on LA DOWNTOWN STREETS.

People intensify their marches. More people come to demonstrate. Writers and actors join the movement, and politicians deliver speeches at street corners. The streets of the United States are filled with protesters. People marches and demonstrations are now similar to political campaign rallies. Consumers' strikes are rowdy but peaceful. People stop buying from businesses that donate and or support Gov-POT- the enablers- across the nation.

AT THE SAME TIME, IN ADAM'S HOUSE, LIVING ROOM.

ROBERT: Ok, I'll work on refining boycott strategies.

MARTA: Elena, I'll work with you on finding international support.

ELENA: And I'll work with the leaders on protest means and methods.

Leaders leave. They have their assignments.
Public Protests Escalate.

IN THE LIVING ROOM. 8:00 P.M.

Elena takes Tim and Sofia to bed. Marta picks up the scattered toys behind the couch.
Robert and Marta, on the couch, turn on the TV.

ROBERT: Elena, dear, come, hurry!

Elena runs to the living room (The TV is on a commercial break). Robert anxiously waits for the news to come back.
Wonders of the Freedom of the Press.
The flow of current situations and conditions brings out a tense situation.
Chain of events.

OUTSIDE ON THE STREET, BY ADAM'S HOUSE. NIGHT.

The marches on the city street intensify. People march around the clock. Reporters walk with the crowd. The silence of the night magnifies their voices, their grieving chanting.

NEWS HELICOPTER OVER STREET BY ELENA'S HOUSE. AT NIGHT.

A P-TV-N helicopter is in the air, and a reporter on the ground with the crowd, linking events at different places, covers the marches. It is exciting, like an action thriller movie. Under attack, people's minds invent ways to survive.

AIR REPORTER: We're witnessing the first-ever candle vigil synchronized over an entire community. Awesome view. It's like a sky full of blinking stars on the ground. Let's go to our ground reporter.

ON THE STREETS.

That percussion sound fills the space, harmonizing with the tempo of the people's marching steps. Amazing, it is rhythmic.

GROUND REPORTER: Here on the ground, the street is illuminated by candlelight. Each person holds a candle. They walk, stop, cover the candles' flames, realign themselves, and, at a specific number and place, uncover their candles, so they spell words with the candle lights, one word at a time. More than a protest march is an awesome light spectacle.

BACK TO THE AIR NEWS

AIR REPORTER: Wow! Yes, you're right. We see the candlelit words, *"Stop unjust arrests." "Stop Illegal Deportations." "Give us our day in court."* Beautiful, never seen before. The marchers repeat this process every five minutes. (Pause) We'll hover around; we'll be back in twenty.

The helicopter flies away and returns after twenty minutes.

AIR REPORTER: The night vigil is underway across LA; it's synchronized. Awesome! What else is happening on the ground?

The ground reporter walks with the crowd. More people keep joining the marches, everywhere, which are becoming parades.

BACK TO THE STREET.

GROUND REPORTER: Here is an awesome, inspiring, and amusing event: people turn their cell phones on and play the same eerie music. Thousands upon thousands of phones on half volume. Marchers stop at every other street corner.

Marchers clear the intersection, opening a space. The space is like a stage. Four masked men, dressed in military gear, enter the stage. The masked men arrest people in the crowd, manhandling and violently tossing them to the ground. They beat them up, cuff and blindfold them, and take them away in less than thirty seconds. The victim's family steps into the scene, kneels on the ground, grieving and pleading mercy, screaming bring them back, they are innocent, law-abiding citizens. The people around bend, arms down to the pavement, then stand up, turn, and raise their arms to the sky. And when the performance finishes, the crowd fills the stage space. The march continues, chanting, '***Justice for All. Give them their day in court.***'

AIR REPORTER: Impressive march; it's a magnificent expression of the American citizens' pain. The world watches the cruelty in the US. Our studio is receiving reports from around the world, including from their television network, which is receiving our transmission. Let's see some of that.

AT VARIOUS CITIES OF THE WORLD. DAY/NIGHT.

London: Thousands of people are on the streets, marching in solidarity with the American people and chanting, "*England respects, encourages, and protects American Democracy.*"

Paris: A large crowd collects at the Triumph Tower, chanting, "*No king, no dictator in the US. Long live the Statute of Liberty.*"

Berlin: People quietly march, just to burst with an angry slogan, "Thank you, America, *for delivering Germany from a criminal dictator. Berliners are Americans in mind and heart.*"

Madrid: People on the streets angrily chant, "*Americans are the natives of the new continent. Europeans who came on and after 1492 are all illegal immigrants.*"

Rome: The Pope blesses the people of the world. Italians on the streets chant, "*God makes all humans equally and gave them the world with love, justice, and liberty, with the mandate to share and care for one another.*"

IN LOS ANGELES.

People fill the streets in all directions. They walk in silence as in a funeral procession. Then, they chant protest slogans, stopping to perform their abduction scenes.

Their protest expresses one clear thought- no one wants to be treated like a possession of nobody else, enslaved in a state of servitude, deprived of all Creator-given, inalienable rights. The evolution of this creation has no room for kings or dictators; they are present only by brute force.

ELENA'S HOUSE STREET. NIGHT.

People mount two huge TV units on a pickup truck back-to-back, facing the street. Marchers can watch TV broadcasts on the street.

GROUND REPORTER: **Breaking News!** The president of the United States just issued an executive order to arrest and prosecute any and all citizens who perform acts disturbing communities' peace and order- Effective immediately.

Perhaps Gov-POT watched and did not like the spectacular demonstrations on the streets and the world's responses. Obviously, he resents seeing the marches gaining momentum, not only in Los Angeles, but across the nation and around the world.

> AIR REPORTER: Military Trucks unload hundreds of National Guard and Marines by the federal building. But the people continue their peaceful, expressive march.

THE FEDERAL BUILDING FRONT. DAY.

CREDUM's lawyers come out of the federal building. Reporters crowd around them, with a burst of questions.

> LAWYER: A minute ago, we introduced a petition to stay the president's order, which violates people's freedom of expression and their right to assembly.

A reporter talks to leaders and marchers?

> GROUND REPORTER: Why are you marching?

> MARCHER 1: Our freedom of expression is a Creator-given inalienable right we must defend.

> GROUND REPORTER: Are you aware of the latest President's order?

> MARCHER 2: It is our right. We will stand our ground to the ultimate consequences. Democracy is based on freedom- no freedom, no democracy, no domestic Tranquility.

MARCHER 1: The Gov-POT is provoking the people, inciting violence. He wants us to riot so the military can attack the people with a justifiable reason.

GROUND REPORTER: There you have it. The people have spoken. Back to the air news.

The people, however, well directed, do not fall into that trap and continue marching peacefully, avoiding confrontations with Gov-POT sicarios.

Public protests are held all over the country.

AIR REPORTER: **Breaking News!** We verified that what's happening here in Los Angeles, California, is also happening everywhere, at the same time. Millions of people are on the streets in 180 US cities, besides Los Angeles.

Government Reaction.

Adam's torturing stops.

Another sequence of events is unleashed by the marches around the clock in Los Angeles.

IN ADAM'S HOUSE, LIVING ROOM. DAY.

Elena, Martha, Robert, community leaders, and CREDUM's representative work on national and local boycott tactics. The consumers' strikes focus on reducing, or completely stopping buying services, products, and or produce from businesses or persons that support the wannabe dictator.

MARTA: Elena, I'm taking the top twenty from the list of American donors supporting the Gov-POT.

ELENA: Robert, schedule consumer strikes on those businesses.

ROBERT: I've set strike durations to two weeks, a month, a quarter, and/or indefinite.

CREDUM-REP: We have drafted a deal for them: strike or stop supporting Gov-POT.

ROBERT: (Screaming) Elena, Marta, come, hurry. The strikes are on TV.

Marta and Elena return to the living room, running.

P-TV-N ANCHOR: **Breaking News!** CREDUM announces consumer strikes: Consumers on strike will stop buying produce, products, and/or services from companies supporting Gov-POT.

In the balance between supply and demand, the formula determines the market prices of goods. But over the years, the free enterprise has abused this equation to satisfy its profiteering. They manipulate supply by controlling services, products, and production availability to raise prices.

The people can apply a similar tactic- stop buying products and or services from selected businesses or persons to reduce and or stop the demand, to reduce or eliminate their revenue. Eventually, bankruptcy will come. We, the people, have the right to buy what we need from sources we choose.

Cameras show on the street, marchers carry signs like, "*This business supports wannabe-king.*" No one comes into or exits from the stores. A reporter interviews a CREDUM officer.

GROUND REPORTER: Sr., please, do you have a strike plan?

CREDUM-REP: We want to show that the big donors should not manipulate our political system. Businesses like Amazon, Tesla, Walmart, among others.

ELENA: Marta, call Justin and Sherlock; they must be ready for Gov-POT retaliation. Robert, coordinate the marchers to stay within the law.

LOS ANGELES STREETS. DAY.

P-TV-N ANCHOR: **Breaking News!** Thousands of strikers walk in front of Gov-POT's donors' businesses, across the nation.

FIVE DAYS LATER.
PRISON CELL, UNKNOWN COUNTRY. DAY.

Adam sits on the damp floor of a solitary prison cell. Two guards come to get him. The door of the solitary, filthy, and stinking cell squeaks open. Adam is sick. He has developed bacteria in his stomach and intestines, suffering malnutrition.

GUARDS: Get up. Get up. You're going to a regular cell. Move.

Adams gets up, but he can hardly walk.

ADAM (POV): This is an obvious move, but the purpose is not. My wife and family must be doing what I would do. Will they release me? No. They won't, but what will they do with me or to me? We'll see soon.

NEW CELL, different prison pabilion. DAY.

A young man, LUIS GONZALEZ, in his late 20s, brings a tray with food, fruits, dessert, and a juice drink. In silence, he opens the pass-through port on the bars' door and shows his ID to Adam. Adam does not understand why. Adam grabs the tray. There is a note wrapped in the napkin written in Spanish, saying:

Note: Soy Luis González, "tu papá es mi tío, hermano de mi mamá, Celina Reyes. Quiero ayudarte."

(Translation) *"I'm Luis Gonzales, your dad is my uncle, my mother's brother, Celine Reyes. I want to help you."*

Adam (P.O.V.): Ah, that's what it is. They want to make me well, giving me better treatment. What will they do with me? I wonder! Could it be a trap? It's possible.

In silence. Adam eats, takes a pen from the tray, and writes. The young man comes back, picks up the tray, and leaves. In the note Adams writes, how do you prove you're my cousin?

Luis goes, but comes back later, when other guards take their afternoon break. Luis dials his mom and passes his phone to Adam. Adam and Celina talk for five minutes; Adam is satisfied with Celina's explanation. So, he trusts Luis, enters his dad's phone number, and passes the phone back to Luis.

ADAM: (Murmurs) Small world, (pause) favorably working for me!

Adam's prison cell is an individual, a single bed, a single cell separated by solid walls on the back, right, and left, bars, and a door at the front. His neighbor prisoners don't speak English; Adam speaks fluent Spanish.

ADAM: Soy Adam Reyes, de Los Ángeles, California, prisionero político. ¿Y vos? ¿Cuál es esta prisión?

(Translation): *I'm Adam Reyes, from Los Angeles, California, a political prisoner, and you? Which one is this prison?*

They converse, whispering in the bar near the dividing wall.

PRISONER 1: Estás en la prisión modelo 2 de San Salvador. Aquí hay solo prisioneros nacionales. Sos el único extranjero.

(Translation)You are in the model prison in San Salvador. There are only national prisoners here. You're the only foreigner.

BACK IN ADAM'S HOUSE, LIVING ROOM. EVENING.

Elena, Robert, and community leaders, along with CREDUM representatives, are in an emergency meeting.
Phone ring. Robert answers, stepping away from the meeting.

ROBERT: Hello, this is Robert.

LUIS: Soy Luis Gonzales, hijo de Celina Reyes, su hermana. Usted es mi tío. Hablé con Adam, su hijo, hoy. Me dio su número de teléfono.

(Translation) I am Luis Gonzales, son of Celina Reyes, your sister. You are my uncle. I spoke with Adam, your son, today. He gave your phone number.

Robert, surprised, quickly tries to understand what is happening. Indeed, he has been disconnected from his relatives in El Salvador. But they talk happily for an hour. Luis gives Robert information about Adam and prison details. Marta and Elena stand around, listening to Adam's news on the phone speaker. Robert hangs up and screams.

ROBERT: HURRAY! They moved Adam from a regular cell.

MARTA: How is Adam...?

ELENA: How... (pause) sorry.

TIM: Mom, you are talking at the same time.

Marta and Elena look at each other, pause, burst laughing.

ROBERT: Adam is ok. Luis says they moved Adam away from other US' political prisoners. It's in a high-security prison model; no information flows in or out.

ELENA: Who's Luis? Does Adam know what was going on here? Is it a tramp?

ROBERT: Luis is my nephew. Adam doesn't know. He thinks they moved him out of confinement because we are taking the right actions; he's proud of you, Elena, and all of us.

ELENA: Can Luis set up a commo channel?

ROBERT: He'll let us know when and how.

They jump with joy, full of hope, but worrying about what could happen to Adam if they find out about his connection with Luis.
Public Protests spread across the Country, following the PFP movement strategy.

A NEWS HELICOPTER HOVERS OVER THE CITY. NIGHT.

News helicopters populate the sky, covering the non-stop marches.

TV ANCHOR: Millions of people march on the nation's city streets. Midterm elections have not started yet, but senators and representatives join the demonstrations, delivering speeches and giving public interviews, unfolding an awesome national drama. They love to have elected officials with them- the way it should be.

At ADAM REYES HOUSE, FRONT PORCH, next DAY.

Elena and Robert come out. The community people, marching up and down the street, stop in front of Adams' house, sitting or standing. News media rush to capture footage.

> ROBERT: Gov-POT is a wannabe king, trying to dismantle our form of government, the rule of law, and our democracy. Our marches and resistance pay off. Gov-POT is retreating, running scared. We'll recover our freedom, government, and our rule of law.

The slow, natural evolution of reality changes occurs as needed, and these changes are caused only by natural elements of reality, such as weather. We do not even notice the changes. The plants grow, the animals live and die, naturally. Ah, but humans do not follow that natural evolution order, the echo systems, the cycle of life. Some human egos are so big that they even believe they are above the Creator. Kings and dictators belong in the egotistic category. Gov-POT, for instance, believes he is above the law, absolutely immune to legal responsibilities. He thinks all powers are his and can destroy our legal system, our democracy, and our form of government.

> ELENA: We, the people, are the only party that can make a more perfect union, if we so desire. Let's make it happen (Pause). Our constitution rests on a concept of government that justifies a revolution when the government openly harms our natural rights. Let's make it happen.

Elena looks up and sighs, her face brightening with hope.
The crowd roars, "Let's make it happen, Let's make it happen."

> ELENA: Let's make it happen; pause, as our forefathers did. Let the freedom bells ring. Let's make it happen. Let

justice shine not for only one, but equally for all. Let's make it happen.

Elena, tears rolling down her cheeks, looks above the crowd to the horizon and then closes her eyes. (P.O.V.) Perhaps it is a dream that may never happen, but it is the American dream. And dreaming is a free hope.

Elena's knowledge flashes back to the beginning of our history, the United States' history.

Philadelphia, 1776. John Adams, Thomas Jefferson, Benjamin Franklin, Roger Sherman, and Robert R. Livingston sit around a desk drafting the Declaration of Independence for a new nation, a beacon of justice, freedom, and democracy for Americans and the whole world. They justify their rebellious actions with grievances caused by a king, an absolute tyrant, who usurps the people's rights. They declare the reasons (quote):

> FOUNDING FATHERS (quote): *"When in the Course of human events, it becomes necessary for one people to dissolve the political bands which have connected them with another, and to assume among the powers of the earth, the separate and equal station to which the Laws of Nature and of Nature's God entitle them, a decent respect to the opinions of mankind requires that they should declare the causes which impel them to the separation."*

Indeed, we, the people, have the constitutional right to charge and remove any government representative by legal means if they violate the mandate of our constitution and disobey our rule of law.

> **ELENA (P.O.V.):** The people had powerful reasons for seeking independence from an oppressive regime (quote continues), then.

> FOUNDING FATHERS (quote continues): *"We hold these truths to be self-evident, that all men are created equal, that*

they are endowed by their Creator with certain unalienable rights, that among these are Life, Liberty, and the Pursuit of happiness."

ELENA (P.O.V.): The committee's list of grievances was convincing, but their solid convictions compelled them to affirm the basis of their rights (quote continues).

FOUNDING FATHERS (quote continues): *"We the People of the United States, in Order to form a more perfect Union, establish Justice, ensure domestic Tranquility, provide for the common defence, promote the general Welfare, and secure the Blessings of Liberty to ourselves and our Posterity, do ordain and establish this Constitution for the United States of America."*

ELENA (P.O.V.): But the Founders' mandate us to form a more perfect Union, which is the greatest requirement vested on us, the people. Let's make it happen.

Elena sighs and looks at the people cheering with joy. Robert steps closer to her, and she makes room for him at the podium.

ELENA: Two hundred and fifty years ago, grappling with terror, grief-stricken people provided reasons for their independence. Today, we, grappling with fear and grief, must provide our own reasons for recalling an abusive president.

ROBERT: Listen to Elena and hold firm to our independence principles, which Gov-POT ignores and undermines through flagrant corruption.

ELENA: Those founding principles that held true then hold true today, as if time has not passed, freezing history until this time. It's our duty to perfect our Union in the next election. Let's make it happen.

ROBERT: Gov-POT wants to be a king or a dictator, having us as permanent subjects, just like King George did. This is our main grievance. Damn dictators.

ELENA: Our constitution is at stake. The president of the United States is taking away our natural rights, attacking us, innocent citizens, with hateful racial discrimination and corruption, placing himself above the rule of law, and consolidating the government branches, as a king.

ROBERT: Gov-POT's intolerable acts and corruption are breaking our republican government and our democracy for his personal gains.

Marchers, with greater confidence stump their right foot to emphasize their phrase, Et Pluribus Unum. They know they are not alone.

ROBERT: But Gov-POT worries about losing what's on the ballot- 435 House seats, and 33 to 35 Senate seats- plus governors, state legislatures, and local officials. Let's make it happen.

MARTA: We, the people, must choose a right cause: Democracy or a King forever.

ELENA: Flip the balance of power to tie Gov-POT's hands, and save our democracy. Let's make it happen.

Robert and Elena leave the podium. Marchers continue to demonstrate their grievances on the streets. Justin is with the crowd and walks towards Elena and Robert.

Justin (P.O.V.): Elena, he calls.

ELENA: Hi Justin, just come in?

JUSTIN: Yes. Pause. Elena, (pause) Ah, nothing. I call you later. Bye.

Meanwhile, IN ADAM'S HOUSE, LIVING ROOM. DAY.

The Global TV Channel is on.

TV ANCHOR: **Breaking News!** World TV Networks shows protest marches against human rights violations in cities like London, Madrid, Rome, Paris, Mexico City, and Buenos Aires; they come out in support of the United States' Solidarity Movement, *'People for People Movement.'*

OUTSIDE KOCH HEADQUARTER, KANSAS. DAY.

TV ANCHOR: **Breaking News!** Armed security guards attack people peacefully marching on the street in front of the Koch building.

AIR NEWS HELICOPTER. DAY.

AIR REPORTER: We report on Consumers' strikes against businesses supporting Gov-POT across Los Angeles.

On the ground: People march on the sidewalks and streets in front of Exxon, Caterpillar, among others, from a long list. Security guards at the Koch building. Security guards throw tear gas grenades at the crowd. People throw them back at them. Guards open fire on the unarmed crowd. City police arrive. One marcher is dead and more than a dozen are injured. Security guards retreat. People return to their peaceful demonstration.

Government Retaliates

OUTSIDE THE WHITE HOUSE, NEWS PODIUM. DAY

The Press Secretary announces that the President ordered the deployment of the National Guard and Marines to quell rising illegal disturbances in major cities.

IN ADAM'S HOUSE, LIVING ROOM.

Elena and Robert come back to the oval table in the living room. The telephone rings. Robert answers on the speakers.

ROBERT: Hello, this is Robert. Silence.

ADAM: Hi, Dad. This is Adam.

Everybody gathers around the telephone.

TIM: Hi, Dad, are you coming back?

SOFIA: Dad, I miss you. Hurry back to play with me.

ADAM: Yes, my worriers, I'll be back soon. Just wait a little bit. I love you. (Pause) Let me talk to your elders.

MARTA: How are you, Adam? We miss you a lot. I love you.

ADAM: I love you, too, honey. Here, things are better now; I think of you all the time. Kisses.

Marta takes the children to their playroom.

ELENA: Dear, we are working hard to get you back. Luis is our voice.

ROBERT: Luis set up a channel, I see. There's a lot we can talk about your case- a day at a time.

ADAM: Elena, Mom, Dad, I don't have much time. I need you to find out about my case in The Hague against the Salvadorean government. Let me know. I love you all. Keep safe, bye.

Everybody says bye. They hang up.

ELENA: Robert, I have to go back to work. Please call Justin and Sherlock. They can help us find an answer for Adam.

LA FEDERAL COURTHOUSE, FRONT. DAY.

Radio and TV news crews anxiously wait for CREDUM lawyers to come out. Thousands of people march around the building. News Helicopters hover over and around the building. Justin Morales and three other CREDUM lawyers come out, and reporters run to capture footage.

P-TV-N REPORTER: Mr. Morales, tell us what actions you are taking in court today?

JUSTIN: CREDUM is suing the US government for violating people's right to assemble and freedom of expression. The President has no authority to deploy National Guard and or combat military soldiers to any city of any state of the United States. Thank you. No more questions.

MARCHERS ON THE STREET.

National Guards march against the people. The Marines march behind the National Guard. The people ignore guards and soldiers and continue their peaceful march, avoiding any confrontation.

IN ADAM REYES HOUSE LIVING ROOM. DAY.

The Adam family was surprised and scared watch the news on television.

ROBERT: This government is, obviously, a dictatorship, but its enablers are worse than Gov-POT, and...

Excitedly, Marta interrupts.

MARTA: Supply scarcity- already here. We must stock up; let's buy essentials and improvise for utility outages...

Cautiously, Elena interrupts

ELENA: But let's keep pressuring the enablers and government.

Robert picks up the phone.

ROBERT: Hello, this is Robert Reyes. You are the candidate for District 30 of Los Angeles County. We'd like you to speak on our demonstration marches, and... (interruption).

Martha, on the other line, pauses it and screams.

MARTA: Elena, I have Cardinal Cunningham on the line. When and where do you like to pray?

Elena gestures on Sundays.

THAT EVENING, ABOUT 8:00 P.M.

Telephone Rings. Elena Answers.

ELENA: Hello, yes, of course. Let me put you on speakers... Go ahead.

JUSTIN (V.O.): Mrs. Reyes, CREDUM has reassigned me to Adam's case. If you want me to, that is.

ELENA: Yes, of course, we need your help.

JUSTIN (V.O.): The Supreme Court clarifies a previous ruling on the President's authority to arrest and deport criminals, but the government must give detainees due legal process and the writ of Habeas Corpus before deporting them.

ROBERT: I heard this before. What's it, a runaround?

ELENA: Robert is right, Justin. Please explain what you said.

JUSTIN (V.O.): The Supreme Court gives the Gov-POT thirty days to bring Adam back and charge him in court, with evidence of the alleged crimes.

ROBERT: Gov-POT laughs at the courts, and the government does nothing.

JUSTIN (V.O.): We'll introduce a motion to present charges and evidence, requesting Adam's presence in court, or dismiss his case. Robert, the President, must comply, or he may be found in contempt of court and in violation of the Constitution.

ELENA: Justin, hold on a minute, please.

Elena, Marta, and Robert discuss the situation and Justin's legal action proposal.

ELENA: Justin, go ahead with these proceedings.

ROBERT: I don't trust the government. This is a delaying tactic, a distraction.

ELENA: Let's use this distraction. Let Justin play it out in court and...

Elena's cellphone rings.

ELENA: Hi! Sherlock, this is Elena.

SHERLOCK (V.O.): Mrs. Reyes, the Salvadorian government will allow a senator and a House representative to visit Adam next week- no date or time has been set yet.

ELENA: That's great news, Sherlock. Do you know who will go to El Salvador?

SHERLOCK (V.O.): We don't know. This is developing very fast. I'll call you as soon as I find out.

ROBERT: Sherlock, can I travel with the representatives?

SHERLOCK (V.O.): I don't think that's appropriate. It's a diplomatic protocol visit.

ELENA: That's ok, Sherlock, thank you for your report. We'll stand by.

The situation is more complex. Elena, Marta, and Robert discuss it. Marta is typing and listening.

DINING ROOM TABLE.

MARTA: It's better for us to stay out of diplomatic actions. I'm afraid of the Gov-POT's biased reactions to Adam's legal cases.

CHAPTER 5

THE WORLD JOINT ELENA'S FIGHT

World Institutions take on Adam's case.

ONE WEEK LATER.

Robert's cellphone rings.

ROBERT: This is Robert. Yes, of course. I'll put you on speakers, is it ok?

GHRP-LAWYER (V.O.): Mr. Reyes, I'm John Cartwright, a lawyer with Global Human Rights Protection (GHRP). The United Nations Human Rights Council, Amnesty International, Freedom House, and Human Rights Watch have retained us to litigate Adams' case. I'll serve as his lead lawyer.

ROBERT: Please, give us a minute.

Elena, Marta, and Robert discuss the surprising proposal.

ELENA: Hi, I'm Elena Reyes, Adam's wife. We are interested, of course. We'd like to know your plan of action.

GHRP-LAWYER (V.O.): We'll represent Adam in world courts against the United States government and foreign governments in connection with his case.

ROBERT: How much will GHRP's services cost us?

GHRP-LAWYER: It's free for victims of government abuse. We'll send you a document. Read, sign, and return it ASAP. Don't delay it. We must act now.

Sleepy, Tim, and Sofia come into the living room.

TIM: Mom, the phone keeps me from sleeping. Mom, is my dad in trouble?

SOFIA: Mom, why so much noise? I can't sleep; cuddle me, please, Mom.

ELENA: Sorry, dear, some friends are working to bring your dad back. Come, let's go back to bed.

Robert set all phones and the TV on low volume. Elena takes the children to bed.
Supreme Court rules on the President's power over raids.

FEDERAL COURT IN SESSION.

A federal judge at the bench.

FEDERAL JUDGE: The Court finds GOV-POT has full authority to deny citizens' birthright to children of illegal immigrants.

ON THE STREET OUTSIDE THE COURT. DAY.

Marchers scream and yell as they march. "*All Europeans who came to America were illegal immigrants. Give us domestic tranquility and Justice for all.*"

IN ADAM'S HOUSE, LIVING ROOM. DAY.

> MARTA: Gov-POT's decision affects millions of citizens-Tim and Sofia.

> ROBERT: Gov-POT attacking children? Damn dictators!

> MARTA: God save America and our democracy.

IN PRISON CELL, UNKNOWN COUNTRY. DAY.

Luis hands Adam his meal with a newspaper under the tray and leaves. Adam reads in silence as he eats.
Adam reads a heading.

> ADAM (V.O.): The International Court in The Hague takes Adam Reyes' case.

> **ADAM (P.O.V.):** Gov-POT is having a hard time. My family is fighting the government to deliver me from this prison.

Adam reads another article as he sits on his bed.

> ADAM: The President signed an order to arrest and deport children born in the US to undocumented immigrants.

Adam's silent rage screams, rattling the prison ward. Armed prison guards run into the prison ward. Adam writhes on the floor, grieving helplessly. The guards open Adam's cell, search, but they find nothing there. Pause. They leave. Luis, nearby, with the tray, the newspaper, and the Adams note, watches but leaves in a hurry.

IN ADAM'S HOUSE, LIVING ROOM. EARLY EVENING.

Robert, Elena, and Marta watch the TV news.

P-TV-N ANCHOR: People react, protesting the Gov-POT order to strip citizenship from illegal immigrants' children.

MARTA: Children of illegal immigrants...

ROBERT: Gov-POT will deport any children he wants to deport. Damn dictators.

NEWS HELICOPTERS OVER US CITY'S STREETS.

Millions of people march protesting in more than 200 US cities-Los Angeles, San Francisco, Chicago, New York, etc.

BACK IN ADAM'S HOUSE, LIVING ROOM.

Sobbing, angry, and frustrated,

ELENA: My children are in danger; (screams) Adam.

BEHIND THE COUCH.

Tim and Sofian play cops and robbers.

TIM: Bang, bang, bang, you're caught, surrender. I'll take you away, to El Salvador, and you'll never come back.

SOFIA: No. Mom said that's illegal. It's not fair. You must let Mom decide. Mom, I don't want to go to El Salvador.

Elena walks to the children and intervenes.

ELENA: Tim, be nice to your little sister. Sofia, don't cry, honey. It's just a game. Stay here with me.

After a short while, Sofia goes back to play with Tim.

ROBERT: Deporting children means deporting their parents. Damn dictators.

ELENA: Correct! Pause. I wouldn't let my children go alone-I'd go with them.

Phone rings. Elena answers the phone on the speakers. Marta and Robert are with Elena.

ELENA: Hello! This is her.

JUSTIN: Mrs. Reyes, I don't want you (all) to panic. The President's order to deport children is harsh, illegal, and it's unconstitutional. CREDUM will counteract. But we need you to make it public. We'll send the basis.

Marta and Robert, listening, gesture to thank him.

ELENA: Thank you, Justin. Robert and Marta also say thank you.

ELENA REYES' HOUSE STREET, DAY.

Neighbors by the hundreds march on the streets by Adam's house, chanting.

NEIGHBORS: (Chant) Justice, justice, justice, For me, for you, for all.

TEN MINUTES LATER.

Robert sets up a podium on the front porch. Radio and TV news crews gather around it.

ELENA'S HOUSE PORCH.

REPORTER 1: Mrs. Reyes, the President is suppressing children's citizenship rights. How does it affect your family?

REPORTER 2: What will you do about it?

ELENA: His order affects my family. And what we will do is within the law.

ROBERT: This order is unconstitutional. We'll rebut it. Damn dictators.

ELENA: My children have a constitutional right to be US citizens.

Phone Rings. Marta walks aside to answer.

MARTA: Hello, this is Marta.

LUIS (V.O.): Tía Marta, soy Luis. ¿Cómo está?

Caption: Aunt Marta, I'm Luis. How are you?

MARTA: Bien, Luisito, espero que estés bien. Espera, tu tío ya viene. Saludos a todos allá. Cuídate mucho.

Caption: Well, Luis, hoping you're doing well. Wait, your uncle is coming. Say hello to all there. Play safely.

ROBERT: Hola, Luis, oí que estás bien.

Caption: Hi, Luis, I heard you're ok.

LUIS (V.O.): Los pájaros llegan en cuatro días.

Caption: The birds arrive in four days.

ROBERT: Gracias, Luis, ahí estaré. Adiós.

Caption: Perfect, Luis, I'll be there, bye,

MARTA: Don't tell me you're going.

ROBERT: Yes, dear, keep it hush-hush.

TIM: Grampa, are you going to see my dad? Tell him to come back.

SOFIA: Can I go with you, Grampa?

ROBERT: Hush, children, I won't see your dad. He'll be back soon. Go on, play. I'll make a phone call.

SHERLOCK (V.O.): Hello, Sherlock at SPIES.

Confused, Robert recalls that SPIES stands for Secret Private Investigation Express Services.

ROBERT: Sherlock, Birds fly south in three days, stargazing in four. Bye.

SHERLOCK (V.O.): Ten four, bye.

Elena returns from work. Marta and Robert are waiting for her. They go over Robert's plan.

ELENA: That's fine. Pause. Just be careful and keep us in the loop.

People use social media and smartphones in the market.

TV IN ADAM'S HOUSE LIVING ROOM.

AIR REPORTER: We see senators and representatives speaking at people's marches. Voice and music are uploaded onto social media through mobile devices.

P-TV-N ANCHOR: **Breaking News!** Thousands of people on the street and millions in their homes throughout the nation turn their cellular phones on to listen to podcast speeches.

ROBERT: Gov-POT can't say it is fake news! This is not a whisper. The world hears the Americans' grievances- their agony.

P-TV-N ANCHOR: Wow! A professional singer and the marchers sing in chorus, 'America the Beautiful. It's an engaging, moving, patriotic moment, never seen or heard before.

THE STREET, FRONT OF ADAM'S HOUSE

P-TV-N REPORTER: Emotionally, people march; they stop, they kneel, they cry, and grieve. They stand, embracing each other, in solidarity with citizens deported to foreign prisons.

IN ADAM'S HOUSE, LIVING ROOM. NIGHT.

MARTA: Amazing. If Adam could see this love and solidarity, he'd also cry. God save Adam, and our democracy.

Elena sinks to her knees, her heart overflowing with emotion as tears stream down her cheeks. She wraps her arms tightly around her children, drawing them into a warm, protective embrace. The warmth of their connection fills the air with unspoken love. In the background, a photograph of Adam rests on a side table, capturing a fleeting moment. His gaze is soft yet contemplative, as if he, too, is sharing in the profound bond of the family before him.

IN JUSTIN'S APARTMENT, NIGHT.

Doorbell rings. Justin opens the door. Elena enters. Justin embraces her, and they kiss while they walk to his bedroom.

IN THE BEDROOM

Hugging and kissing, they undress. They breathe faster and faster. Justin turns the light off.

IN THE KITCHEN.

Elena, wearing Justin's white shirt, makes coffee. Justin embraces her from behind, kissing her neck. She sighs.

CHAPTER 6

BREAKING THE CHOKEHOLD

US Diplomats visit Adam in San Salvador.

THE BEDROOM.

Justin lay in bed, drenched in a sheen of sweat, his heart racing as he stirred from a restless slumber. The dim light filtering in through the curtains revealed the familiar surroundings of his room, yet an unsettling emptiness hung in the air. He glanced around, his breath catching in his throat as he realized that Elena was nowhere to be found. The lingering shadows danced eerily on the walls, a stark reminder that it had all been just a dream, slipping away like wisps of fog in the morning light.

PRISON CELL, SAN SALVADOR. DAY.

Luis delivers breakfast to Adams, along with the "World" ("El Mundo") Salvadoran newspaper and a note placed under the tray, as is customary.

> ADAM (V.O.): Un senador y un representante te visitarán en un hotel dentro de dos días.

> *Caption: A senator and a House representative will meet you at a hotel in two days. You'll be there the night before.*

Adam (P.O.V.): Gov-POT and his enablers are surrendering; otherwise, they wouldn't allow this visit.

Luis returns to pick the tray and note, *"LUIS, Dile a mi Padre."*

Caption: Luis, tell my dad.

As Luis navigated the narrow corridor, a prison guard's keen eyes caught sight of him balancing a heavy tray in one hand. Beneath the tray, he discreetly held a newspaper, its crinkled pages peeking out slightly. The guard observed Luis intently, noting how the young man's gaze flickered between the tray and the printed words, as if engrossed in the stories unfolding on the page. The atmosphere was thick with tension, yet Luis seemed momentarily absorbed in another world, a fleeting escape from the stark reality surrounding him.

IN ADAM'S HOUSE, LIVING ROOM. DAY.

Elena and Robert work hurriedly on the oval meeting table. The TV is on.

ROBERT: Great! The marches are effective.

TV ANCHOR: **Breaking News!** The Gov-POT approval rating is at thirty-five percent before the midterms, a year away.

Marta bursts into the room from the kitchen, her apron fluttering behind her as the delightful news reaches her ears. Caught up in the moment, she exchanges excited glances with Elena and Robert, their eyes sparkling with joy. In unison, they erupt into a jubilant cheer, "Hurray!" The sound of their voices fills the air, a spontaneous celebration of shared happiness that echoes throughout the space.

ROBERT: We'll recover the Congressional majority: the Senate and the House.

MARTA: ... By a super majority!

ELENA: The news media is doing great; our strategies are super effective.

Phone rings. Robert answers.

SHERLOCK (V.O.): Swallows are set to fly south.

Phone rings. Robert answers.

ROBERT: Hello, this is Robert.

JUSTIN (V.O.): Fed court rules: National guards and soldiers' deployment to cities of any state is unconstitutional. Turn on the TV to the Global channel, quickly. I'll call you later, bye.

ELENA: Justin, wait, wait...

Phone call ends.

ON THE TV

TV ANCHOR: **Breaking News!** The Supreme Court upholds a lower court's ruling that found the government violated migrants' due-process rights. The president can't fast-track a deportation process.

ROBERT: A major blow to the Wannabe-dictator. Damn dictators.

MARTA: Great news! We're safe for now.

ELENA: Great! Adam's abduction and deportation were illegal. Adam has a chance to come back.

Community leaders hurried toward the entrance; urgency etched on their faces. Within mere minutes, a tidal wave of notifications surged through the nation as thousands of cell phones buzzed to life, relaying the breaking news. Social media platforms—Instagram, X, Facebook, WhatsApp, Messenger, and several others—groaned under the weight of the overwhelming traffic, their servers straining to keep up. Amid the chaos, paid mobile services remained operational, a beacon of connectivity in the storm. In the midst of it all, Robert quickly dialed Luis, his heart racing as he sought to share the urgent message.

ROBERT: Hi, Luis. Tell Adam: Gov-POT can't deport anybody without due process.

LUIS: Ok. Tío, la visita está hecha.

Caption: Ok, uncle, also, the visit is set.

Robert hangs up. Phone rings again. Robert answers.

SHERLOCK (V.O.): The movie is at five, Rio Tijuana.

P-TV-N STUDIO, LOS ANGELES. DAY, 7: a.M.

Lights on the TV Anchor, sitting behind a moon-shaped desk, with a floor-to-ceiling glass window behind, a view of the business district, and two large wall-mounted TVs on the right and left of the desk.

NEWS DIRECTOR (V.O.): On three, 1,2,3.

TV ANCHOR: **Breaking News!** This morning, one hundred and sixty countries in an emergency meeting in the UNO, Geneva, concur that, *"If the United States becomes a dictatorship, all small countries will lose their democracies. Resolving to review their relations with..."*

A power outage cuts off the broadcast.

ADAM'S HOUSE NEIGHBORHOOD. NIGHT.

The power grid is down; the neighborhood is in darkness. Adam's house has a solar system and has light and power. Mrs. Ortega walks hurriedly down the street with a flashlight.

IN THE LIVING ROOM.

ROBERT: This is not a casual event; it's a premeditated harassment. Damn dictators and their enablers.

Mrs. Ortega comes, holding the flashlight in one hand, a tray in the other. Ryan is by her side. She is trembling, scared, looking back and to the sides. Ryan grins, greeting Tim and Sofia as they run to the playroom.

MRS. ORTEGA: My dear friends, I wouldn't know what to do if you weren't here. I'm so scared. I need your help. (sobs) My emergency generator, (pause) I couldn't turn it on.

ROBERT: Flora, I'll check it out; let me have your house keys.

MRS. ORTEGA: (crying) You guys have been my support since my husband died.

Mrs. Ortega, feeling deeply sorrowful, gazes downward as tears stream down her cheeks. She gently wipes her nose and tenderly dries her face, lost in her emotions.

MEMORY CALL BACK.
22 YEARS BACK.

The rumble of the military C-130 fills the air as it rolls to a stop, its immense tail lowering to reveal a somber procession. Six caskets, draped with flags, are carefully lowered to the ground—each a grim reminder of the lives lost in the Iraq war. Among them is Captain Ortega, beloved husband of Mrs. Ortega. The sight sends a chill through her heart as the ambulances move away, carrying the fallen to their final resting place.

At the cemetery, the atmosphere is heavy with grief. A soldier solemnly approaches Mrs. Ortega and presents her with a meticulously folded flag, a poignant tribute to her husband's sacrifice. She sits in the front row, her heart aching as the sounds of gunfire echo across the quiet grounds, marking the farewell of these brave souls. The melancholic notes of a trumpet play the haunting melody of Taps, enveloping everyone in a deep sense of loss.

As the ceremony concludes, Mrs. Ortega rises, now a widow, confronting the weight of her sorrow. With tear-filled eyes, she walks slowly towards a waiting vehicle, the burden of grief heavy on her shoulders, each step a testament to her love and heartbreak.

"So much sacrifice, (pause) for what? A folded American flag. Does it compensate for my broken happiness and my future life in solitude? Was this war, truly, for our general Welfare and domestic Tranquility?"

She stares through the car window. Outside, everything moves, slurs, blurs, and fades out of sight, at the speed of the vehicle, like the hopes, dreams, and actions of human lives- illusions, passing at the speed of life.

MEMORY CALL BACK ENDS.

Mrs. Ortega shook her head and looked at Marta.

MARTA: Don't worry, we'll help you...

Elena comes with a pitcher and cups on a tray.

ELENA: Here, Flora, drink this tea and take this pill to calm your anxiety.

MRS. ORTEGA: Thank you, Elena, you're an angel.

Robert comes back.

ROBERT: Flora, your generator was just out of fuel. It is running.

MRS. ORTEGA: Bless your heart, Robert, you're another angel. Pause. Excuse me, Elena, I forgot; I brought this apple pie for you guys.

MARTA: Flora, you must have something else that worries you. Can we help you?

MRS. ORTEGA: (tearfully) They took the Garcias away in the early hours of the morning, around 2:00 A.M. You know, the family in the two-story yellow house down the cross street. Jim Wagner shared the news with me. They took their children, Lucy and Chester, and then they just left; they didn't come back. I'm really scared. Who will be taken next?

ELENA: You're not a threat to Gov-POT. You're an army veteran widow, serving the community.

ROBERT: Damn dictator, cleansing the city, pause, the nation; as Hitler did.

MARTA: They don't care about families torn apart that, possibly, will never reunite. And about the kids?

ROBERT: Could be for an organ traffic cartel?

The conversation continues, and faces and body language reveal their fears, frustrations, and worries. Robert and Marta walk Mrs. Ortega and Ryan back to her home.

PLAZA RIO TIJUANA, BAJA CALIFORNIA. DAY.

The plaza is crowded. Sherlock is at the front of the Movie theaters. Robert arrives.

ROBERT: ...Been waiting long?

SHERLOCK: No, I got here a minute ago. Ready?

ROBERT: Ready, let's go.

TIJUANA AIRPORT, BOARDING LINE.

SHERLOCK: We barely made it.

ROBERT: Sorry, I had to help my neighbor.

INT. IN THE AIRPLANE.

ROBERT: Remember, I'm visiting my relatives, and you're my guest.

SHERLOCK: Got it. Let's take a nap.

CONTINENTAL HOTEL, SAN SALVADOR. DAY.

As Robert and Sherlock step into the elegantly furnished lobby of a five-star hotel, they are greeted by the soft glow of crystal chandeliers hanging from the exquisite ceiling. The air is filled with a subtle scent of fresh flowers and polished marble. In a quiet corner, Luis is seated, engrossed in a book, a steaming cup of coffee resting on the table in front of him.

After a few moments, he rises from his plush armchair and strides towards the exit, leaving behind a glossy magazine splayed open on the ornate side table. With a curious glint in his eye, Sherlock swivels around and extends a hand to grasp the magazine. As he flips through the pages, a piece of paper protruding from between the fibers catches his attention, hinting at a secret waiting to be uncovered.

HOTEL SECOND FLOOR, HALLWAY. EVENING.

In the hotel's lively atmosphere, the soft buzz of chatter and the clink of glasses were the only accompaniment. Adam is imprisoned in a room on the second floor. Right outside his door, a guard is keeping watch at the entrance to Adam's suite. The guard, a young guy in his mid-20s, balances professionalism with a laid-back confidence as he looks around the hallway. Luis is chatting with the guard.

As the scene plays out, Robert walks by, dressed sharply in a fitted suit and a crisp tie that catches the light just right. In a slightly dramatic move, he inadvertently drops a fifty-dollar bill, which floats down like a leaf in the breeze. The guard jumps into action, quickly bending down to pick it up, his brow furrowed as if he senses something off. Luis catches the whole exchange, locking eyes with the guard, who calls out to Robert, shifting the tension in the air and hinting at a deeper connection between them.

THE GUARD: Señor, señor, usted botó este billete.

Caption: Sir, sir, you drop this bill.

Robert acts surprised and moved, takes the bill, and speaks.

ROBERT: Su honestidad me impresiona. ¡Se merece un premio!

Caption: "Your honesty impresses me. You deserve a prize!

Robert draws another fifty-dollar bill from his pocket.

ROBERT: Por favor, acepte estos billetes de a cincuenta y pida una cena.

Caption: Please, accept these fifty-dollar bills, and treat yourself to a dinner.

Robert turns and continues walking away to the elevator.

LUIS: ¡Guau! Cien dólares. ¿Qué esperas? Ve a gozar tu cena. Yo cuido la puerta en tu lugar.

Caption: Wow! One hundred dollars. What are you waiting for? Go enjoy your dinner. I guard the door in your place.

The guard leaves. Sherlock shadows the guard. Luis opens the door. Robert enters the room and, motioning, embraces his son. They sob. Robert and Adam have a lot to talk about. Robert calls Marta.

ROBERT: Marta, I'm with Adam.

Marta sets the phone on the speakers, crying emotionally; Elena, in shock, can hardly speak.

MARTA (V.O.): Adam, my son, (sobs), are you Ok?

ADAM: Yes, Mom, I'm fine.

Elena regains her composure.

ELENA (V.O.): My dear Adam, we miss you, we're doing what you would do, as if I could read your mind. The whole nation is concerned and fighting for your return.

ADAM: It's a matter of time. There's so much to talk about. But how are the kids holding out?

ELENA (V.O.): They are fine, missing you a lot. Adam, the Hague Court opened your case. We're waiting for updates.

ROBERT (V.O.): Here, federal courts have ruled in your favor on several issues.

Elena sobs, crying. Marta brings her a glass of water.

MARTA (V.O.): Adam, we feel we're winning.

Elena regains control of herself.

ELENA (V.O.): Adam, national and international lawyers work on your case. We've created a solidarity movement... Hello, hello, pause, damn phone.

HOTEL RESTAURANT, ELEVATORS. DAY.

The guard exits the hotel restaurant and heads back. The Guard takes the elevator. Sherlock loses the guard.

HOTEL SECOND FLOOR, ADAM'S ROOM. DAY.

Luis's phone beats. He opens the room door.

LUIS: Uncle, the guard is coming back.

Robert and Adams go on talking. The guard arrives in the hallway; Luis gives him the key. The guard enters; Adam is sleeping.

Robert meets Sherlock in the Lobby; they walk away.

SAN SALVADOR CONTINENTAL HOTEL. DAY, 8: OO A.M.

A fleet of police vehicles, their sirens silent but their presence commanding, fills the street in front of and behind the hotel, forming a barricade of authority. News media trucks, emblazoned with station logos, crowd the area, their antennas jutting toward the sky as reporters prepare for live broadcasts while cameras roll.

Armed soldiers, clad in military gear and exuding vigilance, form a protective perimeter around the building, their eyes scanning the surroundings with sharp intensity.

Approaching the scene with a sense of urgency and purpose, the US Congress diplomats arrive in a tight group, accompanied by officials from the US Embassy, all dressed in sharp suits. Towering over them, six stoic US Marines stand guard, silently ensuring the safety of the diplomats as they navigate the bustling activity around them.

IN THE LOBBY.

Security is high, with no guests allowed in the lobby. Guards stand at every door. The diplomats sit at a table in the middle. The government TV media comes in. The elevator door opens; Salvadoran guards bring Adam. He is shaved and groomed, wearing neat clothes. The meeting starts.

HOTEL FRONT STAIRS.

At the end of the meeting, Salvadoran government officials and US diplomats came to the podium at the top of the entrance stairs. The US Congress official talks first.

US SENATOR: We thank the government for letting us visit Adams. The meeting was highly productive and encouraging.

US REPRESENTATIVE: We have confirmed Adam's well-being and look forward to bringing him home.

SALVADOREAN FOREIGN MINISTER: Our government wants to keep good relations with the US; we want to resolve this situation as soon as possible. Thank you, that's all.

SALVADORAN AIRPORT. DAY 10:00 A.M.

Congress officials walk directly to the boarding gate, along with US news reporters.

OUTSIDE THE AIRPORT TERMINAL. DAY.

The sky stretched wide and free, adorned with brilliant shades of blue as the majestic United States Boeing 747 roared to life on the runway. With a powerful thrust, it soared into the clear expanse, leaving behind a trail of white vapor as it gracefully ascended. The aircraft navigated the vast skies, making its way home to the vibrant heart of Washington, DC, where stories of politics and history awaited on the ground below.

SALVADOREAN PRESIDENTIAL HOUSE, FRONT. DAY.

SALVADOREAN FOREIGN MINISTER: Good afternoon! Our government respects universal human rights and is committed to ensuring justice for any citizen of the world. The President allowed US Congress officials to visit Adam Reyes, a criminal, held in our prison.

The minister leaves the podium, seemingly annoyed.

ADAM'S HOUSE, LIVING ROOM. DAY.

Marta and Elena are still sitting in the living room, in deep silence. The phone rings, startling Elena and Marta.

ELENA: Hello, this is Elena... Hi, Justin, you're on speakers, go ahead.

JUSTIN: Mrs. Reyes, turn on Global TV at 5:30 P.M. Pacific time; call you later.

Phone rings. Marta answers.

MARTA: Hello, this is Marta... Oh, Robert... Ok. See you soon. (to Elena) Robert and Sherlock will arrive at LAX at 3:00 p.m.

Marta, Elena, and the children wait for Robert. Finally, Robert and Sherlock arrive. They greet Sherlock as a hero and embrace Robert with joy and enthusiasm never seen before. Marta turns on the Global TV channel.

5:00 P.M.

TV ANCHOR: **Breaking News!** Live from The Hague Court of Justice. We broadcast part of the Human rights violation in the case of Adam Reyes, who is imprisoned in San Salvador, El Salvador.

The Salvadoran Prison Warden is on the witness stand, and a GHRP lawyer carries out the interrogation.

GHRP-LAWYER: Tell the court who you work for.

WARDEN: I work for the Salvadoran government.

GHRP-LAWYER: What do you do for the government?

WARDEN: I am the director of the National Model Prison in San Salvador.

GHRP-LAWYER: Is Adam Reyes a prisoner in the prison you direct? If so, what crime did he commit in El Salvador?

WARDEN: Yes, he is. But this prisoner has not committed any crime in El Salvador.

GHRP-LAWYER: No! Why is Adam Reyes in your prison?

WARDEN: My government privately contracted with the US Gov-POT a US prisoner hosting services.

GHRP-LAWYER: So, whose prisoner is Adam Reyes?

WARDEN: Adam Reyes is a US prisoner.

GHRP-LAWYER: Can the Salvadoran Government release Adam Reyes from your prison?

WARDEN: No, my government cannot do that.

GHRP-LAWYER: Well, tell the Court, who in the hell can do that?

SALVADOREAN LAWYER.: Objection! Witness intimidation.

JUDGE: Overruled, continue.

WARDEN: Only the US President can remove US prisoners or revoke this prison service contract at any time.

GHRP-LAWYER: Is your government obeying the universal human rights laws?

WARDEN: In my opinion, we are.

GHRP-LAWYER: Were you aware that the US prisoners did not have their day in court? Did you get a US court judgement?

WARDEN: We assume they did. But no, we didn't get any such document.

GHRP-LAWYER: No more questions, your Honor.

JUDGE: Court adjourns.

EL SALVADOR, PRISON INTERNAL AFFAIRS. DAY.

Phone Rings. CAPTAIN LOUISE VIVIENNE PEREZ DUBOIS, in her late 20s, answers.

LOUISE: Capitan Louise Pérez Dubois.

Caption: Captain Louise Perez Dubois.

WARDEN (V.O.): Acuse en Corte a Luis González por traición y espionaje. Emita una orden de arresto, vivo o muerto, ahora.

Caption: Charge Luis González in Court for treason and espionage. Issue a warrant of arrest, Luis, dead or alive, now.

LOUISE: Sí, Señor, de inmediato.

Caption: Yes, sir, immediately.

WASHINGTON DC NEAR THE WHITE HOUSE. DAY.

Thousands upon thousands of people march, demonstrating discontent with Gov-POT's performance: on Cost of Living, Constitution Defense, immigration, deportation, and abuse of power.

EXT. ADAM'S HOUSE, LIVING ROOM. DAY.

P-TV-N REPORTER: The international court of The Hague finds the Salvadorean Government guilty of violating Adam's universal human rights and has ordered Adam's release, along with all prisoners covered under an illegal prison service contract between the US President and the Salvadorean government.

ADAM'S HOUSE, LIVING ROOM. DAY.

MARTA: So, is that how they serve justice and protect our universal human rights?

Phone rings. Robert answers.

ROBERT: Hello, this is Robert. Hi, Justin.

JUSTIN: Robert, we have great news. The Hague International Court allows us to use its Adams' case documents as evidence in our US Federal Court case. This evidence is essential to win Adam's case in the US.

Elena at the door runs to Robert.

ELENA: Robert, let me talk to Justin.

Robert assents and hands her the phone.

ELENA: Justin, this is Elena. What's the Court schedule?

JUSTIN: Hi, Mrs. Reyes. We have a court date in 30 days. We expect to see Adam in Los Angeles before that date. The government lawyer presents no objection and no motion to delay the court date.

ROBERT: LIARS. I doubt their willingness. We must step up public pressure and consumer strikes. Damn dictators.

Big Businesses Boycott.
People stop buying in stores.

On the TV.

TV ANCHOR: **Breaking News!** The Wall Street Journal reports that over 50 major companies posted losses in the last quarter due to a sales decline.

LOS ANGELES STREETS. DAY.

TV-N REPORTER: We are with the People marching on the streets of LA. They protest the cost-of-living increase, the government's abuse of power, the Adam case, and corruption.

The ground reporter approaches a CREDUM executive marching with the crowd.

P-TV-N REPORTER: People are not buying from businesses that donate or support Gov-POT. Can you comment on why?

CREDUM-CEO: The government works to enrich billionaires while raising prices for consumers and workers.

CREDUM-CFO: Consumers have the right to choose where they buy their services, products, and or products.

REPORTER 2: Which businesses are the ones that consumers are not buying from?

CREDUM-CFO: There are more than two hundred big businesses that support Gov-POT consumers not to buy from. The top donors include Elon Musk, Steve Schwarzman, Chevron, Amazon, Home Depot, Occidental Petroleum, ExxonMobil, WhatsApp, Ameritrade, Johnson & Johnson (pharmaceutical), etc. No more questions.

The interview ends; the CEO and CFO go back to the crowd.

NATIONAL ECONOMIC STATUS.
BIG BUSINESS IN BANKRUPTCY.

TV ANCHOR: **Breaking News!** Anonymous sources report that 10 businesses are seeking to strike a deal with CREDUM. Five others are ready to file for Chapter Eleven or Chapter Seven.

SMALL BUSINESS BOOM.
AT A SMALL BUSINESS. DAY.

People buy services, products, and produce from small local businesses. News reporters interview consumers as they exit.

P-TV-N REPORTER: Why do you buy at this store?

CONSUMER 1: Prices are competitive. They have lower overhead, a small storage capacity, and fresher products with high turnover.

P-TV-N REPORTER: Why do you buy these chairs at this store?

CONSUMER 2: These chairs are made by local craftsmen; they are of good quality and cheaper. Not like the expensive imported items with high tariffs.

P-TV-N REPORTER: Why do you buy toys at this store?

CONSUMER 3: The toys are made locally, have good quality, and are cheaper. Besides, we help the local businesses.

P-TV-N REPORTER: There you have it. People helping people, not enriching monopolies.

People march chanting, *"No monopolies, no business cartels."*

CHAPTER 7

ADAM RETURN TO THE US

THE PRISON IN SAN SALVADOR. DAY.

Adam sits in the prison yard. Another prisoner comes and sits near him, looking down as they talk.

PRISONER 1 (V.O.): Buscan a Luis y a tres guardias más por pasar información al exterior. Están huyendo.

Caption: They look for Luis and three other guards, passing information outside. They run away.

ADAM: ¿Y cómo sabés vos?

PRISONER 1: Oí cuando el director dio la orden de encontrar y matar a Luis y a los otros tres.

Caption: I overheard the Warden given order to find and kill Luis and the others.

Prisoner 1 walks away.

Adam (P.O.V.): This is critical for me, but for Luis is a matter of life and death. I must not think of something to save Luis.

Adam walks, looking for prisoner 1, who sits by the building entrance. Adam sits next to him, looking down, tying his shoe.

ADAM: Hey, if you know how to reach Luis, tell him to seek asylum at the American Embassy.

Adam gets up and walks away.

FIVE DAYS LATER, AFTERNOON.
IN ADAM'S HOUSE, LIVING ROOM. DAY.

Elena, Marta, Robert, and community leaders on the oval table work on editing text for the signs.
Phone rings.

SHERLOCK: Mrs. Reyes, for unknown reasons, Adam is returning earlier than expected. You may come to the LAX, but you won't see him.

AT SALVADOREAN MODEL PRISON 2. DAY.

Adam, worried, sits on the edge of his bed in his cell. The Warden and two guards come and open the door.

WARDEN: Adam Reyes, you're going back to Los Angeles. Think of your family; no one there can protect them from the M13 gangs.

ADAM: But...

WARDEN: Take him away, now.

AT THE LOS ANGELES AIRPORT. DAY. 7: 00 a.m.

Tens of thousands of people wait on Sepulveda and Century Boulevard Adams arrival.

AIR REPORTER: Adam's plane landed. Security agents take Adam from the runway to a hangar. Five vans come out of the hangar, exit the airport through a back gate, and drive away in different directions.

No one knows where Adam is taken. The people moved to downtown Los Angeles, to the Federal Courthouse. The court does not allow Adam to have contact with his family before the case starts.

Politicians suffer boycotts.

ONE WEEK LATER.
AT ADAM'S HOUSE, LIVING ROOM. DAY.

Phone rings, Marta answers.

JUSTIN: Mrs. Reyes, the Court will start Adam's case. It's on Global TV.

IN FEDERAL COURT IN LOS ANGELES. DAY.

COURT CLERK (V.O): All rise, Honorable Cliff Johnson presiding, the Government vs. Adams Reyes. They all sit.

THE JUDGE: The government charges Adam Reyes with illegal immigration and criminal acts. The Defense may present its arguments.

JUSTIN: Thank you, your Honor. We submit a motion to dismiss this case and to release the accused, Adams Reyes, on grounds of wrongful arrest, false accusation, and deportation.

DOJ LAWYER: Objection, your Honor. The government has evidence of the accused's criminal acts.

THE JUDGE: Overruled, continue.

JUSTIN: We submit this video as Exhibit 1A, revealing the government's illegal actions in Adam's unjust abduction, using unrecognized agents dressed as armed bandits or terrorists.

DOJ LAWYER: Objection, your Honor. That video has not been vetted; it could be fake evidence.

THE JUDGE (V.O.): Overruled. Defense may continue.

THE VIDEO STARTS.

`Two masked men, heavily armed for war, jump off a van, violently assaulting and grabbing Adam Reyes on the sidewalk, hit him on the head, bang him against the van, handcuff, blindfold, and shove him into a black, tinted windows van in less than thirty seconds.

Mrs. Ortega Day Care and Preschool in the background. She and her students in the porch, terrorized, witnessed the abduction, screaming and crying. The black van takes off. Two children run to the street, screaming, Dad, Dad. The van speeds off out of sight.

A young woman and a senior couple enter the camera's frame as they run after the van. The female falls, arms raised up to the sky, crying. The van, big engine roaring, speeds away.

THE VIDEO ENDS.

JUSTIN: (Faces the Jury) The children running to the street are Tim and Sofia- Adam's son and daughter. The lady chasing the black van and falls, grief-stricken, on the pavement is Adam's wife, and the senior couple.

Also appearing on the video are Robert and Marta Reyes, Adam's mom and dad. (Pause).

The presumed agents didn't read Adam's rights. And Adam Reyes, a law-abiding citizen, in no moment thereafter, had his rightful day in court. Yet, the government denied knowing him, but deported him to El Salvador, depriving him of his American citizen rights.

The government cannot claim ignorance of this illegal act, nor can it deny its criminal abduction.

DOJ LAWYER: Objection, your Honor. All that is hearsay to mislead the Jury.

JUDGE: Overrule. The Defense may continue.

JUSTIN: Pause. I call Max Schaffer to the stand.

DOJ LAWYER: Objection, your Honor. This witness is not on the defense list.

JUSTIN: Your Honor, we ask the Court to allow the witness to clarify his name, as noted on our witness list.

JUDGE: Objection overruled. Continue.

Max slowly walks with wheeled-walker to the witness stand.

JUSTIN: Mr. Schaffer, tell the Court your full name and any nicknames you may have. Tell the court who you are and what you saw on the day of Mr. Adam's abduction.

MAX: My name is Maximillian Schaffer, known as Max. I live across the street from Mrs. Ortega's Day Care and pre kinder School. I am an American disabled veteran from the Iraq War. I saw everything you showed in the video you showed.

DOJ LAWYER: Objection, your Honor, the witness is overstating his observation.

JUSTIN: Your Honor, the defense asks the court to let the witness explain his statement.

JUDGE: Objection overruled. The witness may explain his statement.

JUSTIN: Mr. Shaffer, are you sure you saw everything shown in the video?

MAX: I am positive, as I am in this Courtroom.

JUSTIN: What and why are you so sure?

MAX: I am sure, because I filmed the video from my front window.

JUSTIN: Thank you, Mr. Schaffer. Your witness.

DOJ LAWYER: No questions, your Honor.

JUSTIN: I call Mrs. Ortega to the stand.

Mrs. Ortega slowly walks, looking from side to side, scared.

JUSTIN: Mrs. Ortega, please, tell the court who you are, what you do, and what you saw on the day they kidnapped Adam Reyes.

MRS. ORTEGA: (trembling voice) My name is Flora Angelique Ortega, known as Mrs. Ortega. I own and manage a Daycare and Preschool facility. I'm a widow of an Army captain killed during the Iraq war. I was with Adam's kids when two masked men, dressed as soldiers, jumped out of a van, brutally beat Adam, handcuffed and blindfolded him, threw him into the van, kidnapped him from the sidewalk in front of my house, and took off in a hurry. The masked men did not read his rights.

JUSTIN: Why were Mr. Reyes' children with you? Do you know the Reyes family?

MRS. ORTEGA: I teach Adam's kids preschool. He brings them every day. I have known the Reyes family for over thirty years.

JUSTIN: No more questions.

JUDGE: The Prosecution may call its witnesses.

DOJ LAWYER: The President has absolute immunity and authority to arrest and deport criminals. We ask the Court to deny the defense motion to dismiss.

JUDGE (V.O.): A President has immunity only for official actions. But the Court will consider your opinion.

DOJ LAWYER: Your Honor, we ask the Court to allow us 30 days to vet and complete our witness list, as the case suddenly began.

JUDGE: I remind the Prosecution that the Court has allowed more than normal time to prepare its case. I will allow no more than fourteen days to submit a complete evidence and witness list. Pause. The Court adjourns.

ADAM'S HOUSE, LIVING ROOM. DAY.

MARTA: What do all of these prove?

ROBERT: It clearly debunks the Government claim that they didn't know about Adam's abduction. The video proves the government lied to the court. Damn dictators.

ELENA: It implicates Gov-POT and the Department of Justice in an illegal, covered-up operation against the people of the United States.

IN SAN SALVADOR PRISON COURT YARD. DAY.

All prisoners are in the courtyard, while guards search the cells. Adam's former prison neighbors, scared, whisper.

PRISONER 1: Adams ya no está aquí; se lo llevaron; nadie sabe dónde. Tres guardias registran su celda; buscan algo; nadie sabe qué.

Caption: Adams is no longer here; they took him away, no one knows where. Today, three guards search his prison cell; they look for something.

Two days before.

In the vicinity of the American Embassy, a group of National Guardsmen noticed Luis and two fellow Guardsmen near a corner store. Just then, a national guard vehicle abruptly halted in the center of the street, its tires screeching against the pavement. The guards swiftly employed the vehicle as an impromptu barricade, its sturdy frame providing a formidable shield against any potential threats. The atmosphere was tense, the air thick with anticipation as pedestrians glanced nervously at the unfolding scene.

As Luis and Louise stepped out of the store, the air was suddenly shattered by the deafening crack of gunfire. Chaos erupted around them, and in an instant, Louise collapsed to the ground, a pained gasp escaping her lips as she fell. Heart racing, Luis swiftly pivoted, grabbing hold of Louise and dragging her back into the relative safety of the store's confines, his instincts overriding the terror coursing through him.

Outside, the two other escapees were locked in a fierce struggle for survival. In a desperate bid, they slammed their vehicle into the National Guard's armored truck with a bone-rattling impact, metal screeching against metal. The guards, who had been valiantly returning fire at Luis, stood helpless as the weight of the vehicle crashed into them, crushing the momentarily stunned defenders beneath the onslaught of the reckless maneuver. The scene was one of chaotic desperation, painting a vivid picture of fear and determination.

Luis and Louise burst from the vehicle, hearts racing, as they sped away in a desperate escape. The roar of engines echoed behind them, the National Guards hot on their trail, weaving through the bustling streets and narrow alleys of the city.

In a moment of urgency, Luis flung open both the passenger and driver doors, anxiety propelling them forward. With adrenaline pumping, he and Louise leapt out, sprinting toward the looming gates of the Embassy, their voices rising above the chaos. "Asylum! Asylum! Asylum!" they cried out, each shout an urgent plea for safety in a world that felt increasingly hostile. The vast grounds of the Embassy loomed ahead, a sanctuary filled with hope amid the shadows of danger that chased them.

The Salvadoran National Guard arrived just a few minutes later, their vehicle rumbling to a halt. The Marines stationed at the entrance, weapons drawn and poised for action, swiftly intercepted the unit, their voices booming with authority: "Stop, American ground, stop!" A tense silence enveloped the scene as the standoff unfolded. Outside, the National Guard members, rifles tightly gripped, took their positions with steely determination, their gazes fixed on the Marines, awaiting orders that would dictate the next moment of this charged encounter.

Back to the present in the prison yard.

PRISONER 2: Mataron a dos. Luis y una mujer de guardia, LOUISE VIVIANNE PÉREZ DUBOIS, lograron entrar en la embajada de Estados Unidos.

Caption: They kill two escapees. Luis and a female guard, Louise Vivianne Peres Dubois, entered the American Embassy.

PRISONER 1: Dicen que Luis forma parte del tráfico de información.

Caption: They say that Luis is part of the information traffic.

ADAM'S HOUSE, LIVING ROOM. DAY.

Elena, Marta, and Robert are gathered with some community leaders around the oval table in the living room. They're all working together and chatting about different community projects.
Telephone ring. Robert answers.

ROBERT: Hello, this is Robert. (pause) Hi, Sherlock. Hold on, I'll put it on speakerphone.

SHERLOCK (V.O.): The consumers' strike is building high pressure on Gov-POT for the coming mid-term campaign. Fourteen big donors stop contributing to Gov-POT. Call you later. Bye.

MARTA: Wow, he must be in a tremendous hurry.

ELENA: Let's find out what's going on. Robert, please, call Justin.

Robert steps into the dining room and calls Justin. He answers.

ROBERT: Hi, Justin, I'm glad I found you...

JUSTIN (V.O.): Robert, let me guess, Sherlock called you, right?

Phone is on speakers.

ELENA: Justin, this is Elena. Tell us what's going on?

JUSTIN: Simple math. CREDUM reports the President's acceptability rating hit a new low, 36%, due to the bad economy.

ELENA: I'll set up a TV interview with CREDUM and send a P-TV-N crew right now.

ROBERT: Elena, the Community leader needs to mount higher pressure on Gov-POT. Let's adjourn this meeting.

DOWN TOWN, LOS ANGELES STREETS, DAY.

TV ANCHOR: Breaking news! Thousands of new people join the marches. We're receiving reports from around the world about the same public demonstrations occurring in their cities. Let's take a watch.

THE WORLD CITIES' STREETS. DAY.

Thousands of new voices raise their voices in protest. People broke their silence. The world hears the pains, grievances, and miseries of the people in the US. They come out from every village, every city, every country to demonstrate their solidarity in support of America's democracy: the concept that all men are created equal and justice is for all. Their countries don't trade with the US government.

NEWS HELICOPTER OVER LOS ANGELES. DAY.

AIR REPORTER: In Los Angeles, the situation is the same as abroad. At night, they write their slogans with candlelight. Every day, marchers act out the abuse of power at every other corner, with cellular music.

P-TV-N REPORTER: On the ground, people pack the streets so tightly that we can hardly walk. Let's interview some of the marchers. Hello. Can you tell the world what you are marching for?

MARCHER 1: We demand our freedom, our rights, democracy, and a form of government. We want no King or dictator. We want no businesses manipulating our government.

MARCHER 2: The wannabe-king is losing; he is not capable of governing. We must get rid of him and his supporters, who work to enrich themselves.

P-TV-N REPORTER: What do you think will happen in the mid-term elections?

MARCHER 1: We'll win. Our democracy will live forever.

P-TV-N REPORTER: There you have it. People expect a change for the better.

FEDERAL COURT IN LOS ANGELES. DAY.

Fourteen days later, in a US Federal Courtroom.

The Court allows Radio and TV crews in the room, this time. The courtroom is packed. Adam is in a bar cage in the back right corner, facing the jury and the public.

COURT CLERK (V.O): All rise, Honorable Cliff Johnson presiding over the Government vs. Adams Reyes case.

JUDGE: On the motion to dismiss this case, this Court, considering legal implicit-explicit fairness, denies it. The government will be allowed to present evidence beyond a reasonable doubt. The defense may now proceed with its arguments.

JUSTIN: The Court is aware of the Hague case, Adams v. The Salvadoran Government, that...

DOJ LAWYER: Objection, that case is irrelevant to our case on hand.

JUDGE: Overruled. The Defense may proceed.

JUSTIN: The Defense submits The Hague's documentation from that case as Exhibit 30B, evidence of the US government's violation of Adam's human rights. The Jury must know that the Hague-Paris Court found the Salvadoran Government guilty of violating human rights.

DOJ LAWYER: Objection, the prosecution requests the Court to strike out the defense's last comment, as irrelevant to this case.

JUDGE: Overruled; the Defense may continue.

JUSTIN: The Jury must know the Salvadoran Government retains USA citizens illegally sent there without due process, court judgments, or an order of imprisonment. Gov-POT's masked agents illegally acted, abducting and deporting Adam Reyes, an innocent American citizen.

The prosecution intervenes several times to derail the defense's arguments. Adam has his gaze fixed on his family sitting in the public section.

JUSTIN: We call Luis Gonzales to the stand.

DOJ LAWYER: Objection. This so-called witness is not a United States citizen, and doesn't speak English.

JUDGE: Overruled. The Defense may continue.

The court provides an official simultaneous translator; questions and responses are given in English. The Court Clerk and the translator swear in Luis. The witness takes the stand.

JUSTIN: State your name, and the type of work you do in El Salvador.

LUIS: Mi nombre es Luis González, teniente primero de la Guardia Nacional de El Salvador, en los cargos de registros y archivos y de casos de prisioneros especiales.

(Translation) My name is Luis Gonzales, first lieutenant of the El Salvador National Guard, in charge of records and special prisoners' cases.

JUSTIN: Tell the Jury the process you follow for new prisoners.

LUIS: Me aseguro de que los prisioneros traigan el número del caso en corte, la sentencia y una orden de prisión, sellada, fechada y firmada por el juez que preside el caso.

(Translation) I make sure prisoners bring a court case number, sentence, and an order of imprisonment, stamped, dated, and signed by the presiding judge.

JUSTIN: Are there exceptions to this procedure?

LUIS: No, no hay ninguna. Es un requerimiento informativo de los derechos humanos universales.

(Translation) No. There are none. It's a required universal human rights information.

JUSTIN: Did you process these records in the case of Adam Reyes?

LUIS: Ninguno, excepto su nombre y tratamiento en prisión, que consistía en quebrar su moral.

(Translation) None, except for his name and prison treatment, which consisted of breaking his morale.

JUSTIN: Did you request his records and court order of imprisonment?

LUIS: Sí. Pero el director de la prisión ordenó ignorar los requerimientos regulares.

(Translation) Yes. But the prison warden ordered me to ignore regular requirements.

JUSTIN: Did you record this exception?

LUIS: Sí. Pero tres días después, fui removido del cargo de archivos. Y continué con el cargo de prisioneros especiales, Adam Reyes.

(Translation) Yes. (Pause) But three days later, I was removed from the office of prison records. I continued in charge of special prisoners, Adam Reyes.

JUSTIN: No further questions.

The judge calls the prosecutors.

DOJ LAWYER: Is the prison you work for in El Salvador a national prison?

LUIS: Sí, así es.

(Translation) Yes, it is.

DOJ LAWYER: Is this prison subject to foreign countries' laws?

LUIS: No, no lo hace.

(Translation) No, it does not.

DOJ LAWYER: So, this prison offers just holding and caring services for prisoners from the United States, correct?

LUIS: Los servicios están sujetos a un contrato privado con el presidente de los Estados Unidos.

(Translation) Those services are under a private contract with the USA president.

DOJ LAWYER: So, there is no need for records. No more questions.

The judge calls the Defense. Justin redirects.

JUSTIN: Is El Salvador a signatory to the United Nations Organization's human rights? If so, does El Salvador abide by the UN body of human rights principles?

LUIS: Sí, es signatario y, según mi conocimiento, respeta todos los principios de los derechos humanos de las Naciones Unidas.

(Translation) Yes, it is a signatory, and, to my knowledge, it adheres to the UN human rights principles.

Justin calls Louise Perez Dubois to the stand. She speaks perfect English.

JUSTIN: State your full name, your occupation, and the reason you are here.

LOUISE: My name is Louise Vivienne Perez Dubois. I'm a lawyer and a Captain in the Salvadoran National Guard. I am in charge of the prison's internal affairs. I requested asylum in the US Embassy in San Salvador because the government is persecuting me with the intention of killing me.

JUSTIN: Tell the Jury why you're being persecuted.

LOUISE: My government accuses me of treason because I publicly denounced the prison Warden's violation of national and international laws, specifically the prisoners' human rights, as in Adam Reyes' case. My signed full declaration to the US Embassy is the reason for my request for asylum.

JUSTIN: We submit Louise's request for asylum as Exhibit 2D—no more questions.

The Judge calls the prosecution.

DOJ LAWYER: We have no questions.

JUDGE: This court adjourns to reconvene at the next scheduled time.

The public screams with joy, jumping. Adam's family stands, eyes and mouths wide open, in silence, shaking their heads in surprise and delight. Robert's look of doubt reveals he doesn't trust the government.

MARTA: (whispers) Elena, do you notice the way Justin looks at you?

ELENA: Yes, and it bothers me, because I haven't encouraged him in any way.

MARTA: Has he talked to you about his feelings?

ELENA: No, he hasn't, and I hope he doesn't. He's a good lawyer, and we need all the legal help we can get.

MARTA: What if he does?

ELENA: My response is obvious. We'll have to look for another lawyer.

ELENA (P.O.V.): I like him; he's a nice guy. Pause. But it's the wrong time, place, and situation.

CHAPTER 8

ALL NIGHTS DAWN TO LIGHT

STREETS BY THE FEDERAL COURT, LOS ANGELES, DAY.

A sea of humanity, unlike anything ever witnessed, streams through the bustling streets surrounding the Federal Court Building in downtown Los Angeles. The air is thick with palpable tension, as anxious murmurs ripple through the crowd. Faces display a mosaic of emotions—hope mingled with fear, anticipation infused with doubt—each person caught in the throes of suspense as they await the jury's verdict. The moment of truth looms closer, heavy with significance.

The court reconvenes.
OUTSIDE THE FEDERAL COURT BUILDING.

A large crowd marches up and down the street, chanting, *"justice for me, for you, for all, let this be true."*

INT. FEDERAL COURT IN LOS ANGELES. DAY.

In the hushed courtroom, the public sits in profound silence, their faces etched with a mix of anxiety and anticipation. Each expression tells a story of hope and dread, as they await a verdict they fervently wish to be just and fair. The tension in the air is palpable, a silent testament to the gravity of the moment.

COURT CLERK (V.O): All rise, Honorable Cliff Johnson presiding over the Government vs. Adams Reyes case.

Elena, Marta, and Robert, anxiously sitting in the front row of the public section, behind the CREDUM bench, hold their breaths. Adam, in the accused bar-cage, exchanges glances with his family members. The jury slowly walks to their seats.

JUDGE: Has the jury reached its verdict?

Everybody turns to the Jury. Adam stands to face the jury.
Adam (P.O.V.): I trust the jury isn't biased.
The public holds its breath.

LONG SILENCE

THE JURY: We find Adam Reyes not guilty of any of the alleged accusations.

Elena, Marta, and Robert stand frozen in disbelief, their hearts racing with a mix of joy and astonishment. Eyes wide and mouths agape, they seem to hold a silent scream that fills the air around them. The crowd, initially erupting in a collective gasp, quickly hushes as anticipation hangs heavy. The Judge, deep in thought, shuffles through the documents on the bench, his brow furrowing as he deliberates the verdict. All eyes are glued to him, the audience vibrating with impatience and suspense.

JUDGE: The evidence shows Adam Reyes was wrongfully detained, deported, imprisoned, and tortured. This Court orders an unconditional release of Adam Reyes within two days.

The public's whispers and murmurs grow louder.

DOJ LAWYER: Your Honor, the Prosecution submits a motion to stay the release of the accused until the Supreme Court hears our appeal.

Silence returns to the courtroom.

JUDGE: Motion denied- The Prosecution can appeal this Court's ruling, but Mr. Adam Reyes must go free. Pause. This Court adjourns.

The people in the courtroom scream. Adams, in the accused's bar cage, sits sobbing and crying. A guard slowly removes his handcuff and chuckles, but walks him back to prison to wait for his formal release. Adam waves at his family, throwing kisses. Elena and Marta embrace each other, crying- though their hearts are full of joy. Robert waves back. Radio and world TV broadcast the outcome to the world. And as the public exits, the judge's words echo in the room.

Welcoming Adam Reyes.
LOS ANGELES STREETS. DAY.

The release of Adam Reyes causes a big commotion on the streets. People marching express their relief and joy, praising the American justice and the rule of law.
Adam's family faces look as if they are waking from a nightmare.

AT ADAM REYES' HOUSE STREET, DAY.

The people excitedly parade up and down the street.

CROWD: (Chant) The people united, cannot be blighted. Our forefathers rose, united in a cause: freedom, no king, no dictator, no autocrat. We want freedom and justice for all.

OUTSIDE THE FEDERAL COURT BUILDING. TWO DAYS LATER.

The crowd screams, cheers, and chants, "Et Pluribus Unum. Justice has prevailed. Et Pluribus Unum. Justice has prevailed."

FEDERAL PRISON, LOS ANGELES. DAY.

A bustling crowd gathers outside the federal prison, energy crackling in the air. Four soldiers stand sentinel at the gate, their faces stoic amidst the palpable anticipation.

Suddenly, the heavy doors creak open, and Adams steps out, bathed in the light of freedom. His family, a whirlwind of emotions, rushes forward, their tears of joy flowing freely as they envelop him in a tight embrace. It's a magnificent reunion, filled with the kind of happiness that only comes from overcoming the unimaginable.

The crowd erupts into applause, welcoming Adam—the hero who stood tall in a chaotic war marked by fear and violence. A wave of mixed emotions washes over him; his heart pounds loudly in his chest, each thud a reminder of the darkness he's left behind.

Although he carries the weight of his past, he finds strength in the warmth of the crowd. With a genuine smile, he waves and offers heartfelt thanks, feeling the power of connection that transcends even the deepest scars of survival.

IN THE CAR ON THE STREETS.

Adams, in the back, hugging Elena, Marta in the front, and Robert, happy and proud, drives home. Tim and Sofia embrace their dad, happy to have him back.

Thousands of people, standing on the sidewalks, scream, cheer, waving at Adam in the car passing by.

ADAM'S HOUSE STREET, DAY.

Another large crowd sings, screams, and dances, showing their appreciation for Adam's contribution to the neighborhood. Radio and TV crews anxiously wait for a possible interview with Adam and his family members.

The house, decorated for a party by the neighbors, exudes love and warmth. The car arrives. The crowd goes wild. Justin and Sherlock are on the sidewalk. Mrs. Ortega is on Adam's front porch with Tim, Sofia, and Ryan. The Community leaders approach the car on the driveway. There is a lot of hugging and handshaking. Adam steps to a podium by the porch.

> ADAM: My dear friends! It's so nice to be back from hell. I dearly missed all of you. But let me take a few minutes with my family, and then I'll chat with you guys. Thank you for this welcoming party.

A live music band set up on the porch grass begins to play. The crowd continues to scream, "Long live Adam," as they dance and sing along with the band. The party is wild.

IN ADAM'S HOUSE, LIVING ROOM. DAY.

Adam, family, Justin, Sherlock, and community leaders walk inside the house. The oval table was still cluttered with books, documents, copies of the Constitution, laptops, and a printer- solid witnesses of their struggles, their fight, their joy.

> ADAM: Wow, it seems you've been working pretty hard. You must be exhausted.

> ELENA: Exhausted, yes, not from hard work, but from the uncertainty of your presence, your health, and your life situation. And now you're back.

ROBERT: Indeed, we missed you. But Elena led us toward your thoughts with the strength of her love. Long live democracy!

MARTA: And I pray for you each hour, each day, never doubting, always hoping you'd be back.

MRS. ORTEGA: We never lost hope, no matter the situation. Somehow, we knew you'd be back.

TIM: Yes, I'm happy you're back, Dad.

SOFIA: I miss you, Dad. Don't leave us alone, again. I get scared.

Marta and Mrs. Ortega lead Sofia, Tim, and Ryan into the brightly colored playroom, where vibrant murals dance across the walls and a myriad of toys beckon for attention.

Meanwhile, at the stately oval table, Elena, Adam, Robert, Justin, Sherlock, and various community leaders engage in animated discussion, their serious expressions reflecting the importance of the matters at hand. The soft hum of their conversation fills the air, creating a lively contrast to the playroom's cheerful chaos.

ADAM: I'm back. The situation has not ended. I'm ready to help you.

ELENA: Now that the Adam case is almost over, we'll focus on marches, consumer strikes, and the coming elections.

JUSTIN: Mrs. Reyes, CREDUM has not closed this case. We must wait for the Supreme Court to rule on the government's appeal.

SHERLOCK: Besides, the investigation of who the masked men are arresting American citizens is ongoing.

ROBERT: I need to help Luis to complete his asylum process.

CROWD: Our consumers' strike schedule is full for the next three months.

ELENA: Adam, we are working on integrating politicians into our marches as soon as the midterms begin.

The meeting goes on. Adam learns what Elena and Robert have been doing. The meeting ends. Sherlock, Justin, and the community leaders leave.

The Hate Wave flows.
EXT. WHITE HOUSE, ROSE GARDEN. DAY.

The place is set up for a press conference. Most reporters sit at the podium, waiting. The president arrives.

GOV-POT: A horrible judge released Adam Reyes, a criminal. The judge doesn't know what's going on. We have appealed to the Supreme Court of the incompetent judge's ruling to return this illegal immigrant to jail, where he belongs.

The reporters shower the president with questions like.

REPORTER 1: Mr. President, are you aware of Adam's case in the Court of The Hague?

REPORTER 2: Have you violated Adam Reyes' human rights?

Gov-POT walks back into the house, ignoring the questions. **Citizen's arrest masked agents.**

EXT. ADAM REYES HOUSE STREET, NIGHT.

Two blocks down the quiet street, a dark van screeched to a halt, and four masked men, clad in tactical gear, swiftly jumped out. They approached a nearby house with urgency, their expressions hidden behind black ski masks. Moments later, as they emerged from the residence, they were dragging a terrified family, handcuffed and blindfolded, with them.

Just as the masked men reached the van, a dozen vigilant neighbors, alerted by the commotion, sprang into action. United by a shared sense of justice, they confronted the intruders and executed a citizen's arrest, their determination palpable in the air. In the chaos, the neighbors managed to rip off the assailants' masks, capturing clear photographs of their faces—evidence that would prove invaluable. The men have no personal identification to prove their identity.

As the sounds of the struggle attracted more onlookers, the local police arrived, sirens blaring. The neighbors handed over the apprehended men, who now stood visibly shaken, stripped of their anonymity. The family, shaken but resolute, decided to press charges against their captors, determined to seek justice for the traumatic ordeal they had endured. Among the crowd, a compassionate lawyer stepped forward, offering to take the victimized family's case and fight for their rights, bringing the perpetrators to justice.

IN ADAM REYES HOUSE LIVING ROOM, NIGHT.

Adam, Elena, and Robert work on the oval table. Phone rings.

ELENA: What? Yes, of course. Ok, right now. Thank you, Justin.

Elena turns on the Global TV channel.

TV ANCHOR: **Breaking news!** Near Adam Reye's house, four masked men, dressed as soldiers, broke into a house, kicking the door open. Citizens surprise and arrest the vandals, preventing a kidnapping. The people handed them over to the city authorities. None of the masked men had identification. An hour later, at the court, a CREDUM's lawyer filed charges against the men with attacking, beating up, and kidnapping a family- father, mother, and two children, and impersonating law enforcement agents.

ROBERT: Intimidation. This government has no limit. Damn dictators.

Phone rings. Elena answers.

ELENA: Hello, this is Elena. Oh, hi, Sherlock.

SHERLOCK (V.O.): Mrs. Reyes, detectives, and police searched their hideout with a court search warrant. These four masked men also kidnapped Adams. I'm sending you a video of the house search. Justin has a copy.

Elena opens her email on her laptop and projects the video onto the big screen.

SEARCH VIDEO.

Detectives and city police step cautiously into a dilapidated four-bedroom house nestled in a run-down area of Los Angeles, just off the bustling intersection of Sunset Blvd and Alvarado St. The air is thick with the musty odor of neglect, and the living room is littered with empty beer cans and discarded rum bottles, remnants of a chaotic night. In the adjacent kitchen, pots, pans, and a mountain of dirty dishes overflow from the sink, hinting at a complete disregard for cleanliness.

As they explore the interior, one room catches their attention—an office cluttered with desks and computers. A long, yellowed sheet of paper hangs prominently on the wall, displaying a lengthy list of names. Some are ominously crossed out, suggesting finality. Among them, Adam Reyes' name sits near the top, clearly marked through, raising immediate questions about his fate.

In a nearby bedroom, the detectives discover a shocking trove: an array of weapons, including handguns, rifles, and an abundance of ammunition. The sight is accompanied by military surplus clothing carelessly strewn across the floor, suggesting a troubling connection to a possible armed force presence. A dining table occupies the center of the room, bearing a battered phone book filled with a multitude of hastily scribbled contact numbers.

An outdoor surveillance camera system, tailored to the location, links directly to a desktop PC paired with a large flat-screen TV, indicating a level of forethought and planning. Strikingly, the house lacks a landline, but a high-speed internet modem and Wi-Fi router are present, signifying the occupants' reliance on modern technology.

After careful documentation of the scene, the police meticulously confiscate the laptop, desktop computers, and the phone booklet, in addition to the cache of weapons, all entering evidence for what might become a significant investigation. As the last officer steps through the door, he motions to Sherlock, a renowned private investigator who has chosen to remain behind, eyes fixed on the ominous clues scattered throughout the residence.

END OF VIDEO.

ROBERT: The government is a Mafia. Damn dictators.

ADAM: Excellent work, Sherlock.

Phone rings. Robert answers with the phone on speaker.

ROBERT: Hello, this is Robert. Hi, Justin.

JUSTIN: Hi, Robert. CREDUM submitted that video to the Supreme Court. The hearing is in a week from tomorrow, at 9:30 A.M.

ADAM'S HOUSE, LIVING ROOM. DAY.

Adam and family come out to the porch. The crowd screams and cheers.

ADAM: I thank you for your solidarity and support given to my family in this struggle. I'm back, but I come not to rest but to fight alongside you, the wannabe dictator. I'm here to work with political candidates on the coming midterm election campaigns.

REPORTER 1: What can you tell us about your experience in a foreign prison?

ADAM: It was a sad, horrible experience. But this is and will be over soon, so we must leave the past rest. We must focus on getting rid of the wannabe dictator who wants to destroy our country and democracy.

REPORTER 2: Do you have a plan of action?

ADAM: No, I don't. I will follow and support what's already in motion. Thank you, no more questions.

Adam and his family member go back inside the house.
LUIS AND LOUISE RECEIVE ASYLUM.

AT LOUISE RELATIVES' HOUSE FRONT PORCH. DAY.

In Baton Rouge, Luis and Louise sit in rocking chairs, chatting under the covered front porch, which has a veranda and a set of steps down to ground level. A two-story house, with a balcony on the second floor overlooking the street.

LUIS: It is a dream to think I'm in the US. In this tranquil oasis of freedom (sighs). But I dreamed of this all my life- to make it to California.

LOUISE: I'm not surprised you say that. My mom lived here. She went to work at the US Embassy in El Salvador. She spoke English, French, and Spanish.

LUIS: How come your name is Perez?

LOUISE: My mom met my father, a lawyer in San Salvador. But when President José María Lemus was overthrown by a military junta, in a shootout in downtown San Salvador, they accidentally killed my mom and Dad. I'm a victim of a dictatorship.

LUIS: What did you do?

LOUISE: I had no choice but to stay with my dad's family. I inherited all my mom and dad had. And I study law.

LUIS: And how did you get involved with the Salvadoran National Guard?

LOUISE: I wanted to find out the truth about my parents' death. I had mixed feelings; I wanted to come back to America.

LUIS: What did you learn?

LOUISE: My mom and dad were killed by accident in the crossfire. (pause) And what is your story?

LUIS: Short. I got a government scholarship, but I had to join the National Guard. I study business administration.

The sun slowly sinks below the horizon, and the lights on the street come on. Louise and Luis went back into the house.

IN ADAM'S HOUSE, LIVING ROOM. NEXT DAY.

Phone ring. Robert answers.

ROBERT: Hello, this is Robert. Pause. ¿Hola Luis, donde estas?

Translation: Hola, Luis, where are you?

LUIS: Hola, tío, estoy en Baton Rouge, en casa de unos parientes de Louise Vivienne. Mi sueño de venir a vivir a los Estados Unidos se cumplió.

Translation: Hi, uncle, I'm in Baton Rouge. I'm at Louise Vivienne's relatives' house. My dream of living in the United States came true.

ROBERT: ¿Qué quieres decir?

Translation: What do you mean?

LUIS: Nos van a dar la tarjeta verde, la visa de residencia permanente. Pensamos mudarnos a Los Ángeles.

Translation: They are going to give us the green card, the permanent resident visa. We are thinking to move to Los Angeles.

ROBERT: Bueno, piensa bien tus pasos. Y si necesitas ayuda, avísame.

Translation: Ok, take your steps well. And if you need help, let me know.

LUIS: Gracias, tío. Yo le aviso. Hasta pronto.

Translation: Thank you, uncle. I'll let you know. So long.

ROBERT: Está bien, adiós.

Translation: Ok. Bye.

A WEEK LATER, 9:00 A.M.

At 9:30 A.M., after the Supreme Court ruling today, Adam and his family sit in the living room. The TV is on, commercial break. Doorbell rings.

OUTSIDE, at THE DOOR.

Mrs. Ortega and community leaders stand at the door. Marta opens the door.
Marta hugs Flora and greets the leaders.

MARTA: Hi, come in. Adam and Elena wait for you.

Flora brings a basket full of freshly baked biscuits. The aroma fills the air and whets the appetite. Elena hugs Flora and, with Marta and Flora, walks to the kitchen. Adam and Robert stand and greet the community leaders.

ADAM: Just in time. The Court is about to deliver its ruling.

They all sit around the oval table facing the TV on the wall. Marta, Mrs. Ortega, and Elena come with the biscuits, a pot of coffee, and cups. The TV returns from commercial break. Elena pours them coffee.

ON TV.

JUSTICE: The Court has studied your written arguments. I call the DOJ lawyers to present their arguments.

SILENCE.

DOJ LAWYER: FBI Agents under DOJ order found Adam Reyes to distribute false information to destabilize the government. Adam is born to an illegal immigrant from El Salvador, and is a member of the M-13, a terrorist gang...

JUSTICE: You are repeating your written theory. Please present additional evidence that proves your written argument.

DOJ LAWYER: Honorable Justice, our written argument is sufficient cause to arrest and deport Adam Reyes, because he represents an imminent danger to the president, the nation, and citizens. But we may add that Adam Reyes conspired and subverted three agents of the Salvadoran national guard, creating a shootout in which two guards were killed, and two entered the US Embassy in San Salvador- evidence of Adam Reyes violent character. We have no more evidence.

JUSTICE: The defense may present its arguments.

JUSTIN: Honorable Justice, the Defense has already rebutted each point of the DOJ's argument. But we will add. The United States granted protection to a young student,

Robert Reyes, persecuted with the intention to kill him for publicly protesting the abuse of power of Salvadorean Government of Lieutenant—Col Julio Adalberto Rivera in 1966. We also submit a letter of asylum granted to Robert Reyes by the USA. We add the International Court of Justice's ruling as evidence of Adam's human rights violation. We also add the USA letter of asylum for Luis Gonzales and Louise Vivienne Perez Dubois as evidence rebutting the accusation of illegal instigation to subvert the Salvadoran government.

JUSTICE: Having heard the DOJ and Defense's additional arguments and received new evidence, this recesses until 2:00 P.M. This afternoon. Session adjourns.

The high murmur rumbling in the room buffers the public words. But the public wonders about the outcome.

OUTSIDE THE FEDERAL COURT BUILDING.

A large crowd marches, chanting "Et Pluribus Unum, Et Pluribus Unum." People united demonstrate that civic activism can inspire hope and change for all.

ADAM: If the Supreme Court goes by the truth of evidence, we'll win.

ROBERT: I wonder about Gov-POT's influence on the Supreme Court.

ELENA: CREDUM's lawyers presented a strong case. People also strongly influence possible outcomes.

MARTA: My dear son, life and liberty are pending on dark probabilities.

AT THE SUPREME COURT.

1:00 P.M. THE COURT RECONVENES.

Adam's family and leaders return to the oval table.
The TV goes on.
There is a profound silence in the courtroom; everybody is holding their breath, anxiously awaiting the outcome.

JUSTICE: This Court finds the DOJ failed to prove its case. The Defense's overwhelming evidence exonerates Adam Reyes. We want you to feel confident in the fairness of our justice system.

OUTSIDE THE FEDERAL COURT BUILDING.

The people demonstrating burst into an overwhelming scream of joy and satisfaction, their cheers echoing through the streets. They dance, embrace, and celebrate a victory that feels beyond human emotion, waiting for CREDUM lawyers, their heroes who defeated the wannabe-king.

GROUND REPORTER: We're here on the street with the people. This is wild. There is no chance to talk to anyone. Their emotions have captured their minds. We'll wait until their overwhelming joy comes down.

IN ADAM'S HOUSE, LIVING ROOM. DAY.
ON THE TV, P-TV-N.

The government appealed to the Supreme Court, presenting unreliable and or unsubstantial evidence in the case.

P-TV-N ANCHOR: **Breaking News!** The Supreme Court denies the appeal and upholds a federal court's ruling that the government lacks authority or justification to keep Adam Reyes in a foreign prison.

LOS ANGELES STREETS. DAY, 9:00 A.M.

Throngs of people surge through the streets of downtown Los Angeles like a tidal wave, a scene of unprecedented fervor. National Guards and Marine soldiers stand at the ready, their weapons poised, creating a formidable presence alongside the passionate marchers. The air buzzes with energy and determination, making this moment truly unforgettable!

IN ADAM'S HOUSE, LIVING ROOM. DAY.

Elena, Marta, and Robert are in a meeting with Community leaders.

ROBERT: (to the leaders) Try to get the moving stages' guard rails ready for tomorrow.

FEDERAL COURT IN LOS ANGELES. DAY.

In the case of Gov-POT mobilization of troops to the streets of cities of the states of the Union, the court holds its final hearing.

The JUDGE: This Court finds the federalization of National Guards and mobilization of combat troops to cities of any of the States in the Union is unconstitutional. This court orders the immediate removal of guards and marines from Los Angeles and any other city.

Midterm Campaigns start.

TV ANCHOR: Public demonstrations against Gov-POT and his enablers are taking place in every city across the nation. And now that the midterm campaigns have started,

Democratic candidates are speaking and marching with huge crowds.

Elena runs for House representative.

The community leaders of Los Angeles' central district nominated Elena Reyes as their candidate. Elena now not only leads the crowd but also speaks for a constitutional society. Elena talks to her family.

ADAM: Honey, the people want you. You're their hope, their leader. You must be with them. I'll support you.

ROBERT: You see, things always happen for something that is coming. You can take it as a signal or a message, of which you can see the result at the end of the cycle of causes. Take this opportunity.

MARTA: Elena, you got what they need: guts, courage, and knowledge. Besides, if you've done it from the outside, from the inside, you'll do even more, I'll vote for you.

Elena ponders her decision for a while, then stands and walks to the porch. The community leaders are waiting.

ELENA: When we are split, they win. But when we, the people, stand together, we WIN! I accept your nomination to work with you for our shared future.

Adams leads the marches.

Adam and Robert, the brilliant strategists behind Elena's campaign, have teamed up with CREDUM to craft impactful objectives that will advance her vision. Together, they're on a mission to elevate Elena's message and make waves in the campaign world!

The Supreme Court orders the Government to stop illegal arrests and deportations.

Elena is with the marchers in her district. The telephone rings. She answers.

ELENA: Good morning, Justin. I'm on the street with the marchers.

OUT OF THE MARCHERS' STREAM.

JUSTIN (V.O.): Mrs. Reyes, tomorrow morning, the Supreme Court will rule on the government's power to deport US citizens. Watch it on Global TV at 10:00 A.M.

ELENA: Yes, of course. We'll do. Thank you.

FEDERAL COURT IN LOS ANGELES. DAY. 10:00 A.M.

A sprawling crowd of thousands gathers outside the imposing Federal Court building, their faces a mix of anticipation and anxiety. Among them stand Adam, a determined young man with tousled hair; Elena, a fierce advocate with a clipboard; and Robert, an older gentleman whose lined face reflects decades of experience. The sun sets behind the towering structure, casting long shadows as they anxiously await the announcement that could change everything. The atmosphere buzzes with murmurs and whispers, a palpable tension hanging in the air as the reality of the moment sinks in.

JUDGE: The court finds that all arrests and deportations must be legal. All persons, citizens or not, must have legal representation and be charged in a court of law. Thereby, this Court orders the return of all deported individuals to the USA to have due process.

ROBERT: The most significant setback for Gov-POT. He won't comply—damn dictators.

ELENA: Gov-POT faces a difficult civil and political situation.

ADAM: He has no playbook rule he can apply. He's trapped, finished.

Gov-POT is far behind the Democrats in the polls.

P-TV-N REPORTER: **Breaking News!** Gov-POT lost his big donors. His current approval rating is below thirty-two percent. ZNN (Zoom National News) and NAH (News as Happens) report that voters are turning away from the Republican Party. They now forecast democrat landslides in all races.

ADAM'S HOUSE STREET. DAY.

A large crowd of well-wishers and supportive neighbors gathers in the streets surrounding Adam's house. As Elena, Robert, and Adam arrive, their hearts swell with gratitude. Justin and Sherlock step out of their car, and the moment is electric with joy as the crowd erupts in cheers and screams, warmly welcoming these heroes they admire so much.

NEIGHBORS: Elena, Elena, Elena. God's miracles saved Adam. May God save the US.

TV and Radio reporters move to the front, looking for a better location. Adam, Elena, and Robert walk to the house porch. The reporters shower them with questions.

P-TV-N REPORTER: How do you feel to be back, free and sound?

REPORTER 1: What do you plan to do now?

REPORTER 2: Do you feel safe, Mr. Reyes?

ADAM: Too many questions at once. I'm happy to be here with you, with my family. I'm ready to continue with my life, in the safety that our democracy provides. And I'll join you in the work ahead.

P-TV-N REPORTER: Mr. Reyes, having gone through what you have, what's your take about our government?

ADAM: I'm a law-abiding citizen, not a politician. But my take is that (pause), this nation, every state, belongs to us, the people. Our democracy, our form of government, and the rule of law belong to the people. None of these belongs to politicians. Those we elect to represent us in the three branches of our government must defend and protect our Constitution.

REPORTER 1: What is the role of those elected to run the government?

ADAM: The role of those we elect is to manage our government according to our will and wishes, according to duties written in the Constitution. We don't surrender our nation to the politicians we elect.

REPORTER 2: We almost had a dictator for years. In your opinion, how can we prevent that?

Adam looks tired. Elena and Robert step in.

ROBERT: I'll answer that. Our Founding Fathers explicitly stated it in the Declaration of Independence in 1776. The people don't want to be ruled by another king, ever, nor do they want to be controlled and manipulated, divided, by an autocrat, nor a dictator, never. And when this situation arises, we, the people, have our constitutional right to change that government.

ELENA: We just went through this situation. And now, we the people, must make a more perfect union, where such a situation never arises again to threaten our democracy, our constitution, our rule of law, our pursuit of happiness, and the blessing of freedom and justice for our posterity and us. No more questions. God Bless America and the people.

Adam, Elena, and Robert walk inside the house—the crowd outside cheers and screams.

CROWD: E pluribus unum. People united cannot be blighted—liberty and justice for all.

The chanting goes on for the rest of the day, and at dusk, the people leave the streets- a silence representing the domestic Tranquility restored.

FOURTEEN DAYS LATER.
EXT. DODGERS' STADIUM. DAY.

The community leaders and CREDUM hold a celebration of democracy and the form of government, Adam's return, Elena's win in the House, and Luis and Louise's wedding. The Dodgers' stadium is complete. Several live bands played in the celebration for most of the night.

In the middle of the field, there is a large table. Adam's family, Luis and Louise, community leaders, Sherlock, Justin, CREDUM representatives, and some politicians sit at the table.

A priest performs the marriage of Luis and Louise, and the couple leaves in a limousine waiting. The limousine leaves through the stadium back gate under the scoreboard.

STADIUM BIG TV SCREENS.

Mrs. Ortega and Ryan stand in the middle of the field. Ryan's family, arrested and deported by unidentified agents, returned to the US. Mrs. Ortega welcomed this family and returned Ryan to their parents.

THE AFTERMATH.

ON THE STADIUM SEATS.

The TV flashes on Adam's deported neighbors: The Miller family, The Fonseca family and their teenagers, The Garcia family, who live in the yellow house. The flashes continue, bringing images of citizens deported who are now in the stadium seats. The celebration goes on. Around midnight, a global TV channel announcement appears on the big field TVs.

> TV ANCHOR: **Breaking News!** We have been informed that the last group of deportees has come back to the United States to have their day in court.

The audience screams louder than when Shohei Ohtani hits a home run with three runners on base. And the echo of the night carries that scream of relief, and joy...

> The people in the stadium seats chant in harmony: "Adam, Adam, Adam." Adam gets up and walks up the platform.

ON THE PODIUM.

A profound silence envelops the stadium. Adam stands looking up and around.

> ADAM: I'm humbled by your courage, determination, and solidarity. You've given a new life, thank you. You save our

democracy, thank you. You have discovered a new leader, my wife, Elena. Because with you, everything is possible. But I also thank a great lawyer, Justin Morales. Justin comes up here.

Justin stands, turns around, and bows to the audience. Walks to the speaker's platform.

JUSTIN: I'm honored, though I don't deserve it. I don't deserve it because I just did my job. But I admit that I was inspired by a woman, grief-stricken, who dared to stand her ground when everything appeared lost. I fell in love with her. Pause.

Marta and Elena look at each other. Elena lumps in her throat. Just open a Pandora's box, and she can't control what Justin will say next.

JUSTIN: Yes, I fell in love with her courage, with her determination, and her vision, her willingness beyond grievance, to fight a mighty force, and she overcame, and with the people's support, she brought back her beloved husband, Adam Reyes. Thank you, Elena, for allowing me to work with you and for helping me discover a new dimension of commitment in the face of adversity.

Elena relaxes; her frantic feelings had no reason after all.

ADAM: I now call my wife to the podium.

Elena slowly walks up to the speaker's platform. Adam and Justin grab her arms and help her step up. The audience stands applauding for long minutes.

ELENA: Thank you, pause, thank you, thank you. I...

The applause continues. Elena waits, looking at the audience in the seats and on the field. The audience sits down. Two men walk through the crowd, carrying large video cameras; they were a batch hanging from their necks.

> ELENA: We, the people, have been caught between two forces: a government that no longer works for the general Welfare, and a greedy free enterprise. A free enterprise that has enslaved us, the people, in a consumer society that feeds their ambitions and greed. And we let them get away with it.

The audience stands up, applauding for another three or four minutes, then sits.

> ELENA: Our government has been corrupted, and now it doesn't work for us, the people- now it works for the greedy free enterprise. And we let them get away with that.

The audience stands up, applauds for another three minutes, then sits. The two men lift their cameras on their shoulders to start filming the event.

> ELENA: These two forces have brainwashed us to take what they feed us without question- fashion, entertainment, and social media. They heard us like sheep on their path. We let them get away with this. They manipulate the market and the law of supply and demand, prices, and movie genres. We let them get away with that, too. They turned the iPod, smartphone, and smart TV into marketing and sales billboards. They charge us for their service. We let them get away with that, also.

The audience stands up, applauding for two more minutes, then sits. The four men with cameras are approaching the podium.

ELENA: It is time that we take the reins of our lives, our destinies. Let's dictate how we want to live our lives the way we want, and yes, we can get away with that; it's our right. God bless you, and save the United States. Thank you.

The audience stood up, applauding again, but this time they started chanting.

"Et Pluribus Unum, Et Pluribus Unum, Et Pluribus Unum. We, the people, united, cannot be blighted. (Chant) Unite, unite, unite. The people united cannot be blighted. Unite your force with ours. Unite for just one cause. Unite to have a better life."

ADAM: Now, please, for those two Salvadoran National Guards who gave their lives to make my return possible. Let's light the candles by your seat, and turn the stadium lights on for one minute, while we pray in silence.

The stadium organ plays "America the Beautiful," and at the end, the live bands start the celebration.

A deafening series of gunshots shatters the air, echoing ominously throughout the stadium. Panic surges like a wild tide as people on the field race toward any exit they can find, while spectators scramble to shield themselves, desperately searching for safety in the chaos.

Amidst the turmoil, Adam, Robert, and Elena hit the ground, instincts taking over. Nearby, Marta drops to her knees, eyes wide with fear. The crowd, in sheer panic, overwhelms two camera operators, dragging them down into the fray.

In the midst of the chaos, a doctor in the crowd springs into action, pushing through the crowd to reach the podium. He kneels beside Elena, quickly assessing her injury. A bullet has grazed her arm—a shallow wound, but enough to send shivers of fear through her. Adam lies motionless, a bullet lodged in his chest, his breathing a silent plea for help. Robert, too, is down, blood seeping from a wound to his head, his survival hanging by a thread.

Moments later, sirens wail as ambulances and police cars flood onto the field. Paramedics rush to Adam and Robert, urgency driving their every move. Marta, clutching Elena as they board the ambulance, glances at her bandaged arm—a reminder of the chaos that has turned their lives upside down in an instant.

The stadium lights go off. The crowd lights their candles and starts praying for a minute.

And so, the plans, the dreams, and the glory of a tremendous victory vanish. An empty stadium remains in silence.

End of Story.